How to Make Your Money Work

DECIDE WHAT YOU WANT, PLAN TO GET THERE

Eoin McGee

Gill Books

Gill Books
Hume Avenue
Park West
Dublin 12
www.gillbooks.ie

Gill Books is an imprint of M.H. Gill and Co.

978 07171 9367 7

Design and print origination by O'K Graphic Design, Dublin
Edited by Djinn von Noorden
Proofread by Ciara McNee
Printed and bound by CPI Group (UK) Ltd, Croydon CR0 4YY
This book is typeset in Adobe Garamond Pro 11/17 ptt.

A CIP catalogue record for this book is available from the British Library.

5 4 3 2 1

How to Make Your Money Work

Eoin McGee is a financial planner, the founder of Prosperous Financial and the host of RTÉ's *How to Be Good with Money*. His first book, of the same name, is a number-one bestseller.

In memory of Dad, who had more impact on my life than any other man ever has or will. I love you.

Michael A. McGee

10/6/1942–7/12/2020

CONTENTS

INTRODUCTION

Why write another book?

My first book, *How to Be Good with Money*, was a tour of your finances: it was the concepts, the ideas and stuff you needed to know. Many of you who read it got so much from it, but when I finished it, I knew I needed to add more. The first book was all about how to be good with your money; this book is about your interactions with your money. Not only the practical steps to be taken in what you do with it, but also about what may be underpinning your deeper relationship with money – the *why* behind the things you do with it.

I wanted to write a book that lets you into the mind of a financial planner, that allows you to understand how we think and why we do things differently for different clients. I wanted to do this in the hope that you could read the book, learn from others and decide how you need to take action with your own finances.

And I want it to be the right action. So many of us look at what others are doing with their money and try to do the same. But, inevitably, we get different results. Why is that? It's because what works for one person may not work for another. When dealing with a client's finances we often apply different strategies, and it's no different for you: what works for your best mate may not work for you. There is more than one way of getting ahead with your finances and creating wealth.

This book aims to help you find your way – the specific financial path that

1

works for *you*. If *How to Be Good with Money* was the **what** to do, *How to Make Your Money Work* is the **how** to do – and **why** we do it.

What I've learned from the people I meet

Since I wrote my first book, my life has changed in many ways. For one, the book has been a phenomenal success; for another, I have finished three series of the TV show *How to Be Good with Money* and, as I write, series four has just been given the go-ahead. I have broken through my 20-year professional milestone of advising clients – and have also broken the 40-year age barrier.

I'm still constantly learning from the world around me. What I love about what I do is that there is so much I have yet to learn, and I'm delighted with the fact that this will always be the case.

I learn from my clients, from people on the TV show, people who ask me questions on radio and now I also learn so much from my interactions with people on Instagram. In Ireland, we are not good at talking to each other about money. I feel as though I'm doing everything I can through the TV show, the books and both traditional and social media to get people talking about money – or at the very least to talk to *me* about it. It seems to be working. I do it because I love it, but I also do it because I learn from it.

For example, I was doing an Insta Live recently. If you're not familiar with this, it basically means turning on my camera and broadcasting live to my followers, who in turn join me live with their followers. It's like a mini interactive live TV show.

Others who have lots of followers think I'm mad ('Sure you could have anybody join you', 'You have no control over what might be said', 'What if they ask you something you don't know the answer to?'). My response to this is always the same: 'That's why I enjoy it so much.' It's the privilege of being let into somebody's home. Somebody's life. They can open up a bit and really give everyone watching this mini TV show an insight not just into their finances, but into their lives.

During an Insta Live, people can also throw up questions or comments for everyone to see, and to me this is where the real value and learning comes from. I had somebody who wanted to buy a house recently. It was a dream home; the price was good and it was in the right location. But there was a problem: the seller wanted to delay the sale for six or eight months. Their solicitor was advising them to pull out, as it was 'just too risky'. I was on the spot. My suggestion was to drag things out, keep looking at other houses and see how far they could hold off before pulling out. Yet I felt for the seller, as I was suggesting that the buyer lead them along, but I also felt that the buyer was being put in a crappy position.

That's when the magic happened. Someone suggested that the person buy the house and rent it to the current owners for the few months they needed. And what was really weird is that this is something I have done before with a client – but in this moment I had gone a different route with my suggestion. This is the power of collaboration. Yes, this option is not without its faults, and the bank in particular may have an issue, but it was an option to at least explore.

We all need to learn from this: there is usually more than one option and it's about deciding which is the right one for you, while also acknowledging that the right answer for somebody else may not be *your* answer.

I've added an FAQ section at the back of the book so that you can see the kind of questions that come up over and over again. I'm privileged in that I get to look at lots of different scenarios for lots of different clients. I learn about lots of different people's lives, situations and problems, and then I take that knowledge and use it to help others.

I'm always learning: I'm always reading books, listening to podcasts or watching documentaries to try and make sure I can give better solutions to my clients and the people I engage with through social and traditional media. But without doubt my greatest asset is the people I engage with.

Lessons from lockdown

It's not just my world that has changed since my first book came out; the whole world has changed. We've experienced a global pandemic and our perspective on life has been turned upside down as a result. As we went from lockdown to lockdown, we began to realise that there were things we really missed.

I really got into Instagram during the lockdowns and the feedback I received from polls has given me a great insight into people's minds. When I asked people what they were missing during lockdown, one answer kept coming up over and over again: people were missing people. Some expanded on this and said going to restaurants with people, going to a bar with people, spending time with people, staying in hotels with people, travelling with people.

When we were stripped of our ability to engage with the world, what we missed most was each other. We tried to replace it with things like Zoom drinks, but that only lasted so long. Zoom dating had some, but limited, success. People, not things – and definitely not money – were what we craved and what we missed.

As my Insta journey unfolded throughout lockdown, I also got to partake in the evolution of people's relationship with their finances. While people were missing their friends and family, they also realised there were things they were not missing at all. Whatever about deciding there are people you don't want back in your life, that is your own decision, but finally recognising that there is stuff in your life you don't need was a eureka moment for me.

For years now I have been fighting against the pre-conceived idea that financial planners are 'tight'. Let me dispel that myth right now. Financial planners are not penny-pinchers, they are not tight, they do not scrimp and scrape and they do not sacrifice today for the benefit of some far-off future financial euphoria that may never come.

Good financial planning is about not spending money on things that add no value to your life in order to have more money for the things that do.

The eureka moment – for not just Ireland, but for the entire western world – that arrived during lockdown was that there is whole pile of stuff we spend our money on that adds absolutely no value to our lives. I have previously described this as subconscious spending. Lockdown meant if we wanted to spend money, we had to do it very consciously. Even if we went to essential shops like the supermarket, it was a chore: there were queues, and we were concerned about getting in and out as quickly as possible. Cutting our subconscious spending had a major impact on all our household finances. Yes, there were also other factors such as not commuting to work or not going out to eat or drink, but the impact was significant.

In a typical non-pandemic month, the people of Ireland save an average of €443 million. In the month of April 2020 – the first full month of lockdown – we saved €3,000 million. That's €3 billion. In one month we saved almost seven times as much as we usually do.

If you saved more that month than you usually do, I'd suggest you didn't land at the end of the month feeling like you had missed anything tangible. I know this from my Instagram polls: we didn't miss tangibles in lockdown. We missed our friends, our family and the people we love.

This figure is even more incredible when you consider unemployment figures during April 2020. The total workforce of Ireland is approximately 2.32 million people. Just over 200,000 were on the live register in April 2020 and another one million were either on the Pandemic Unemployment Payment or on the wage subsidy scheme. Yet we saved seven times as much as we usually do. Think about it: we saved as much in one month as we usually save in almost *seven* months, yet 1.2 million people were either out of work or on some type of government support.

There are other figures that, when you look further at them, suggest there are two million people in Ireland who are financially better off as a result of Covid. Their wage stayed the same (including via PUP or wage subsidy), yet their expenses and subconscious spending fell through the floor. These are the savers.

How to use this book

If you've read my first book then you know it's full of tips, hints and recommendations about how to engage with your money. You'll also know that I say you can jump in and out of it and just read the bits that are relevant to you; I do recommend that you read it cover to cover, but that was an option if you were short on time.

This one could potentially also be read in bitesize chunks – but you'll miss a trick. Money is intertwined into different areas of your life, so what you do with one area of your finances will have an impact on others. You need the full picture. Or as any politician would say, you need to have joined-up thinking when tackling something.

So do yourself a favour and read this book cover to cover. After all, you don't know what you don't know yet.

WHY IS MONEY IMPORTANT?

Right, first things first. Money is important because when we have some it allows us to do the stuff that we want to do. It allows us to spend time with family and friends, it allows us to buy nice things, have experiences and enjoy financial security.

This is a really interesting question. Why is money important to you? Some people say, 'It's is not important to me, I'm not materialistic.' If this is you, and if you believe that money is not important to you, then ask yourself – why haven't you given all your money to charity? Why hold on to it if it's not important to you?

You might answer that you need it for food and a roof over your head, nothing more, and therefore it's not important to you. Saying it's not important, however, is the same as saying eating isn't important: it is. So is money. We need money for essentials, therefore it *is* important. I find it fascinating to think back to a time when money did not exist, when we actually didn't need it. We didn't need it because we foraged or hunted just enough to feed ourselves and our family, tribe or community. As the available food in an area disappeared, we simply travelled on to the next area and kept looking for food.

But then we started to travel more, and the size of the population increased. People became skilled. Somebody began growing food but needed the tools to carry out the work required. In stepped the craftspeople, who made tools and equipment and traded their products for food.

Now, if the world only had craftsmen and farmers in it, then our need for money would never have developed. You see, trading between two people or two communities can be done very easily when each person has something the other person wants. The reason for this is twofold. The first is basic need. I'm hungry and you want my tools. Simple. But the second is that it's only my perception of the value of your item that is important to me. So my judgement is the most important. If I perceive that my tools are worth two bags of grain, then I'll give you the tools. If I don't, I won't – and we barter until we are both happy.

Where it starts to get more complicated is when I'm selling you my tools and in return you're going to give me a bag of grain. But if I don't want the grain and intend to use it to barter with the baker in the village, now it's not just my opinion of the value of the grain that matters – I need to consider what value the baker will put on it. The baker is not here, so I have to guess. I could guess right or wrong.

But what if I had a system where I could get something for my tools that nobody questioned the value of, where there was a universal value to it? Something that was trusted. Something like money. Then I wouldn't need to worry about my perception of how the baker might feel about two bags of grain this week.

But for money to be acceptable to all, it needs to be trusted by all. Notice I said it needs to be trusted by *all*, not just some people. So in years gone by, the king or ruler or whoever it was who reigned over a region would issue coins with their mark on them, effectively providing a 'government' guarantee of their value. It meant I could accept coins for my tools and use those coins in the bakery, safe in the knowledge that the king was standing over its value. The baker knew that too and so the baker could go off and buy grain or whatever else was needed.

In its simplest form, money meant three-, four- or even five-way transactions were possible. But it needed somebody standing over it saying, 'It's okay to trust these coins.' The modern-day version of this is our regulators such as the European Central Bank and the US Federal Reserve.

Right now, though, we're living in an era where this is being challenged. I genuinely have no idea where, for example, cryptocurrencies will go. In ten years from now – or even by the time you read this book – they could be totally established as an accepted form of currency everywhere. Or, in the same period of time, they could have become useless. At the time of writing, cryptocurrencies are on a rollercoaster of a ride; for now, all I'll say is that my one major concern about current cryptocurrencies is that, in order to become fully mainstream, they will need to have the trust of everyone. In all likelihood, this means being regulated. And if a central bank or regulator is going to do that, why would they not simply create their own cryptocurrency, rather than trust one created by someone else? So it's possible that crypto may become a thing of the future – but it may not be the one you're currently holding.

What money can do for us

Having asked thousands of people the question 'Why is money important to you?' over the years, I have come to the conclusion that money is important because when we have some it allows us to do stuff we want to do. It allows us time with family and friends, it allows us buy nice things, have experiences and enjoy financial security. It allows us to provide for our children and it allows us to make decisions that we wouldn't be able to make if we had none.

When we get new clients into the private practice who have just won the lotto, sold their business, inherited money or in some other way come into a large, life-changing amount of money, we try to get one message across to them. That message is: the things that made you happy before are the things that are going to make you happy in the future, the difference now is you have more time to enjoy those things.

We can always earn more money. We can never make more time.

Money is important because it gives us time. Time to spend with family or friends, time to experience nice things, places and events. Time away from worrying about money. Having money does not make you happy, but it does give you more time to do the things that *do* make you happy, and having lots of money means you might do things with your time in a more comfortable way, in nicer restaurants, hotels or via better seats on the plane. But only if they are important to you. Managing the money you have is all about a mixture of balance and trade-offs.

I'm a financial planner. An accountant looks backwards at your finances and tells you where you are today. A financial planner views where you are today and then looks forward. When I sit with a client for the first time, I show them what their financial future was going to be like before they sought financial advice. For many clients, this is the first time they see with real clarity where they are going financially. But more importantly than seeing where you were going, you can also see where you could go if you make changes. You get to see the long-term impact of the financial decisions you're making today.

This can be really powerful: it helps you avoid the situation where you wake up 10 years from now and wonder to yourself, *If I had done that differently would it have worked out differently?* You can see now what your financial future looks like, based on the decisions you're about to make.

A good financial plan means that you can enjoy today more, safe in the knowledge that your financial future is secure. A good financial planner, however, does more than generate a good financial plan. A good financial planner will delve deeper, will understand what is important to you so that they can build a financial plan that has your money working hard to support the life you want to live.

Yes, it's about financial security in retirement and yes, changes may need to be made, but these changes are not sacrifices. Suggesting you're sacrificing something suggests you're at a loss. But proper financial planning means you don't sacrifice – you trade off to achieve balance.

You decide to save a little more now so that you can spend a little more later on, or you trade off the pay rise and increased responsibilities at work in order to keep your work-life balance right. You don't move house but instead extend, because you realise that moving house means you'll have to work for three extra years to cover the cost of it, while the extension means you'll only have to work one extra year.

Life is full of trade-offs – some are financial, but there are also trade-offs in our decision to stay home and watch TV rather than go out with friends because that is just what we feel like doing; or eating boiled rice instead of fried rice so we can live a healthier life in the future. The realisation that financial trade-offs are no different than the other trade-offs we have in life can help us to recognise that looking after our future by changing what we do today is not a sacrifice; it's a choice. We are in control of it, and we do it to improve our overall life experience.

Cutting things out can sometimes be hard, but cutting things out in order to have more time, more money or a better future is empowering. Every time you put some salary into a long-term investment or a pension, or each time you don't buy something that adds no value to your life, means you're changing your decisions today to gift yourself a better future.

What is our relationship with money?

Our relationship with money can be deep-rooted, and often stems from influences we're not consciously aware of – whether that's our upbringing, our culture, our life experiences or things we see in the media around us. Later in the book I'll introduce you to my six money personalities – Fionnuala Fear, Gerry Greed, Helen Hurry, Liam Later, Conor Clueless and Brenda Brilliant – the general categories into which most people roughly fall in their financial dealings. I wonder if you have a sense, just from their names, of which money personality is closest to your own? But just because we've always thought one thing doesn't mean we always have to. Changing our thoughts around money helps us to change our relationship with it. The first thing we must realise in relation to our money is that we control it – it does not control us. And this is never more prevalent than when somebody loses their job.

I have spent time with people who have lost their job. If you have been made involuntarily unemployed before, you might recognise what I'm about to describe. If you haven't, I want you to imagine how it might feel.

You're working away and things, you feel, are going well. Then something like Brexit or Covid hits, and all of sudden your boss tells you there is no more work. It hits hard. People tell you that 'it's not your fault' – and you agree, you know you were not responsible for Brexit and you know you didn't cause Covid, but you still feel awful. Or if you lose your job for other reasons, and still people tell you it was not your fault: it was the economy, it was bad management, it was a decision that was made at a desk with the swipe of a pen thousands of miles away. Often they're right, and sometimes you hear these things being said to you, sometimes you listen. Other times you can't help but think, *Maybe it was my fault, maybe I could have done this better or this differently*. It's an incredibly difficult time, and a point in many people's lives where they question their own self-worth.

Your money mindset

Nobody has more of an impact on our financial education than our parents. We observe our parents and their relationship with money and we decide, either consciously or subconsciously, to be exactly the same or exactly the opposite to them.

If you're not sure which applies to you, then consider your attitude to debt. Whenever a client comes to me with the goal, 'I want to clear my mortgage as soon as possible', I can reasonably assume that when I delve just a little, I'll discover the reason for this desire is in their upbringing or in something that happened with their parents and money when they were young.

Inevitably when I probe with the client, I'll ask them to put their goal to one side for a minute and tell me what their parents were like with money. The story then usually goes one of two ways: either their parents were riddled with debt, they were swamped and couldn't manage at all, it was awful to be around, there was never any money in the house and they don't want to be the same. Or it will be that their parents didn't borrow for a single thing and always saved for whatever they wanted and never overstretched themselves. Although these two scenarios seem very different, they aren't. They both reflect parents who hated debt; they just hated the debt for different reasons.

Debt is an easy one to examine and to establish the traits that resulted from what you witnessed as a child regarding money. Do you save for stuff or just buy it and worry about the financial consequences later? Do you feel okay about spending money on yourself or do you not feel entitled to do so? Little events in our life can have an impact later on. Was there something you really wanted as a kid and couldn't have? Was there always that underlying feeling as a child that there was no money in the house, or even the opposite – that there was no issue with money and that it grew on trees?

You also need to consider how the adults in your life as a kid interacted with each other and with you about money. Assuming you grew up with both your parents, did they discuss money openly or was it taboo? Was it a traditional home where Dad worked and gave Mam the money to manage? Did Mam have little envelopes of cash stashed all over the house? Or was it the other way around, that Dad had all the money and Mam had to go asking if she 'needed' anything?

To be honest there is an entire book to be written – probably co-authored with a psychologist – around our parents and money. For now, I just want you to think about your upbringing and consider how it might have influenced your thinking today around your relationship with money. What are you carrying from the past, and is that having a positive or negative effect on your relationship with money? We'll come back to this later, when we look at the key financial habits adults and children alike should learn.

Power and control

Let's go back to considering the point of losing your job. Regardless of the reasons why it happened, there is that moment that you arrive home, sit down and you think to yourself, *I don't know when I'm next going to get paid work.* It feels as though you have lost control. You know you have social welfare coming in, but you don't know when you're going to be able to get back into work and get paid for doing something. It can make you feel helpless, but more than anything it can make your feel as though all your power and control has been taken away from you.

When I'm talking to people in this situation, I always ask them to do these simple things. I ask them to sit down with a pen and paper, check how much money they have in their bank account today and work out when their next social welfare payment is coming in. I then ask them to figure out what expenses they have between now and then.

When they have done that, I ask them to allocate the money from their account to cover each of the expenses. If they don't have enough, I ask them to prioritise what must be paid. If there are absolute essentials such as food that can't be covered, I ask them to contact their mortgage provider or their other lenders to see if they can get some leeway.

Believe me, the difference between calling your bank and asking for a break on your loan repayments after having made those calculations versus calling the bank before making the calculations is incredible. If you've done this task, and you know you can't afford to put food on the table without a break on your mortgage, it feels more like a courtesy call. Your attitude becomes, 'I'm either feeding my family or I'm feeding you, Mr Banker, and guess what – I prioritise my family', as opposed to ringing them, cap in hand, asking for their help.

Often you discover that you still have control over your money; that it doesn't control you. When you feel like you have lost control over your future because your job has been taken away from you, these small wins can be incredibly important. But everyone needs to realise that this is not just something you should do if you get let go; this is something we should all be doing every single month. Several times a month, in fact.

Love and money

Losing your job can have a significant impact on your other relationships too. In fact, whether you lose your job or not, our relationship with money has a serious impact on our relationships in general – particularly our romantic relationships.

From the first date, money can be a serious bone of contention. All you have to do to see this is watch programmes such as *First Dates* and observe the interaction between a couple when it comes to paying the bill. Obviously I'm looking at it with my financial-planner glasses on, but I do find it fascinating.

Taking a heterosexual couple: if he pays, she is either absolutely delighted and feels like a princess, or else the feminist in her comes out and she wants to know why he doesn't see her as his equal.

Then you have the women who insist on paying and the man either jumps in with, 'Only if I can pay next time.' To be fair, it's a smart move when either side of the table uses that one, because it avoids that awkward moment later when you're sitting beside each other and asked 'So, do you want to see each other again?'

Alternatively, he insists and she feels put down or diminished in some way.

Then you have the couple where one suggests they go halves and the other agrees, only to find the camera panning to the one who made the suggestion looking downcast that it was accepted. It's a minefield and very entertaining to watch this financial interaction, but getting it wrong can ruin a first date and mean there is no second one.

Unfortunately, there is no right or wrong here; it's a couple's preference as to how this is going to pan out and what works for them. What doesn't work, however, is when two people in a partnership have opposing attitudes towards money. Opposing views over who pays can be an easy excuse on a first date for why there won't be a second, but in the long run, romantic partners need to adapt and compromise in terms of how they deal with their finances, particularly if these come to be shared. And that is all down to good communication.

Confirming and surviving

We do this a lot in life. It's called confirmation bias. We make our mind up about something and then we look out into the world to find reasons to confirm that we are right, while conversely we ignore the reasons that confirm we were wrong in our decision.

For example, I'm not a fan of investing in the shares of just one or two companies. I much prefer to be boring about it all and spread my clients' portfolios across 5–6,000 companies. In other words, I like to diversify.

From time to time I'll have a new client come in to me who has an extremely concentrated portfolio of shares in a very small number of companies. This is when they become competitive. They ask how my portfolio has performed; I try to resist because when I do, they ultimately go on to compare the apple to the orange and explain to me that their shares are significantly outperforming my portfolio.

This is where yet another behaviour bias kicks in: survivorship bias. Survivorship bias is effectively evolution – it's the idea that the strongest survive and the weakest don't. It's the same with the client's current concentrated stock portfolio. They have shed the losers and are now getting confirmation that all their selections have been brilliant because they are only looking at their winners; their losers have been sold and are no longer in their portfolio. So when they are looking at their winners they are thinking (confirming) to themselves that all is good and that they are winning.

Reality check.

The hard truth of the stock market is that something doing really well in the past is not necessarily an indication of where it is going in the future. For example, take the US stock market: when you look at the companies that manage to make it into the top 10, they will have to have performed better than the average stock market company. That makes sense; they wouldn't be the top companies if they weren't above average.

Sometimes people who buy shares in individual well-performing companies feel that the run is going to last forever. The stats tell us differently: 10 years before a company breaks into the top 10, they perform better by 10 per cent per annum compared to the entire market. Narrow that down to three years before they make the top 10, and on average they are outperforming the market at a rate of 24.3 per cent per annum.

That's phenomenal – and if you were to know this in advance you could outperform the general stock market by almost 25 per cent per year for three years.

The problem, however, comes next, at a time when your confirmation bias is high and you might even now have some sort of an emotional attachment to this company because it has done so well for you. The stats are now against this company, and it is likely to underperform the market in the coming years. In fact, on average, three years after a company gets into the top 10 based on its financial size it outperforms the market by 0.7 per cent, but give it 10 years and, again on average, it will have underperformed the market by 1.7 per cent per annum.

Companies may still give you good returns over the long term, but I find that when people are hand-picking shares in a small number of companies they are keen to get on to the next big thing. The statistics above show that once the company reaches top-10 status it's likely to underperform in the overall stock market over the long term. This means that the stock-picker will want to move on, resulting in them needing to double down on their bets. They have to bet that it's the right time to get rid of their current stock as well as identify and bet on which share is going to be the next big thing. It becomes a minefield, which is not navigated well by professionals – never mind the person who does it part-time from their phone.

To link back to our relationships, confirmation bias happens on dates too. If you really like the other person and want to see them again it won't matter to you who pays. If ordinarily you expect the other person to pay, you offer to pay and they accept but say, 'I'll get the next one,' with a little wink. You'll still be pleased with their not paying because of the suggestion of another date. On the opposite end of the spectrum, if you subconsciously don't want to see the other person again and they leave you to pay, that may be the issue you consciously use as your dealbreaker.

Early in a relationship it can be very easy to let confirmation bias dilute your own needs, beliefs and wants. Some people might describe this as thinking with your heart and not your head. But be careful – as with everything else in a relationship, you create habits early on, including financial ones. For example, if your partner always pays and that's how it has always been, when you move to the mid-stage of the relationship and they stop paying or start to ask you to go halves, that might be a bit of a shocker. Do they not love me anymore? What has changed? you might ask yourself. You need to be aware of your own confirmation bias early in a relationship if you want to see the relationship last.

Financial dynamics

As a relationship develops, money can become a serious stressor. If one person earns significantly more than the other person, it can also be an issue. The person earning more money is happy to pay to do things because they want to do nice things and they want to do them with you.

To begin with you might try to keep up with them financially, but if the wage gap is significant enough you may find over time that you start to pull back from doing things because you simply can't afford to do them. If communication between you both is poor and they don't know why you're pulling back, they may be justified in jumping to other conclusions as to why you don't want to go out anywhere with them anymore. If you do come clean and explain that you just can't afford to keep up then it becomes a tightrope walk: either they try to persuade you that it's okay, or they think you're playing them to get them to pay for everything.

Don't underestimate the significance of a big wage gap in a relationship. This is exacerbated at certain times of change too, such as when you decide as a couple that one person should give up work to mind the kids, or one person loses their job, or gets promoted and all of a sudden becomes the main earner. These are all times of financial change, which can become times of financial stress. The dynamic shifts completely. Often it's easier for the person who is in the 'positive' position to help sort out this situation before it becomes a problem.

If you're the one staying at work while your partner gives up their job to stay home with the kids, you need to realise that some, if not a lot, of their self-worth likely came from what they achieved at work. There are similarities with being made redundant in that they have also lost their ability to earn and may feel worried about being able to provide for themselves. In addition, no matter how strong your relationship is with each other, don't be surprised if they feel uncomfortable about spending 'somebody else's' money on themselves, particularly for non-essentials. (Although don't get me wrong, this isn't what happens to everyone – some people will be more than happy to spend your money!)

The 'staying home to mind the kids' situation is probably an easier conundrum to fix than the redundancy issue. In this case, it's about the person working realising the value of the stay-at-home parent. Ultimately, of course, it's up to your family and your budget to determine this value, but there are a number of studies out there that can provide a reference point to start with. Articles on independent.ie and irishmirror.ie respectively named stay-at-home 'salaries' as being worth €44,000 (in 2019) and €50,000 (in 2020), for example.

Let's just accept that minding, feeding and driving the kids around, coupled with the housework and all the other things, does have a significant financial value if we were to assess it. But there is also the support that it gives you, the 'at work' parent, to chase career opportunities, go to required work events and possibly the extra sleep you get because things are done for you at home by your partner.

Once the working parent recognises this, they should pay for it. Yes, the one-income household means the working parent pays the bills, rent or mortgage and all the other family costs, but I see it as being very important that they also pay a 'wage' to the stay-at-home parent. This confirms the value you place in what they do, it allows them to have their 'own' money to spend and sets a level of recognition that goes beyond the odd, 'It's great you're at home all the time.' If you have a stay-at-home partner, understand that they are working. They are working in the home, and they should be paid for that. The amount they are paid is actually less important than the recognition that they deserve a wage; and what's most important is the communication between you both.

If you're not in a couple, there are also important takeaways from this lesson. You need to be paid your 'own' money too. If you're working hard, paying your bills, paying the rent or mortgage or saving for a goal in the future, you also need to ensure that you have some F money. (You can decide if 'F' stands for 'fun money' or 'fook-it money'.) The point is that you need money that you can blow guilt-free, safe in the knowledge that everything else is looked after. If you don't pay yourself, as it were, you'll very quickly be questioning the point of it all.

Another area that couples can really struggle with in terms of wage gaps is when one person gets promoted and significantly overtakes the previous breadwinner. This gap in earning capacity can be one of the trickiest to navigate. It should be a time of joy: the family just got a pay rise and the old breadwinner will obviously be very proud of the other person and their achievement, but they have also just been dethroned. Some people will take it in their stride, but others won't. The reality is that, whether you're male or female in a heterosexual or homosexual relationship, we all assume financial roles in a couple from the very first date. We have our jobs and if your job has been as the provider, the hunter-gatherer, then losing this job can make you feel at worst insecure, worthless and unsure of your purpose in the relationship. Throw a little bit of unwanted jealousy and some resentment in there, and you could potentially end up in a position where this niggle becomes an actual problem.

The thing to accept here is that this is an actual issue, a real one. Not just a niggle. The research I have seen only looks at a male–female relationships, but it established that seven out of ten adults found it 'very important' for the man to be the breadwinner if they were to be a good partner or husband (us men can be quite insecure when it comes to our female partners earning more than us). It's also believed there is a sweet spot. Splitting expenses 50:50 isn't even good enough for us: our sweet spot, the research suggests, is if women contribute 40 per cent of the household expenses.

I'm a bloke and like to think I'm quite modern, and this research does surprise me. But to defend men in this instance, I do believe that this is primarily driven by societal beliefs and not necessarily individuals coming to these conclusions on their own. What's worrying about the research for men is that when the financial imbalance is out of sync and our female partner is earning more, it has shown to result in physical health issues such as high blood pressure, heart issues and unhealthy dietary and exercise routines. Granted, the research may be taking a whole pile of ordinary male health concerns and hanging them on one issue, but it's an eye-opener all the same. The sad thing is that if this is how society as a whole feels about how male–female earnings should be split, then is it any wonder we have wage-gap inequality between men and women? Perhaps society, and especially men, should consider this and realise that fixing the wage-gap issue would result in fewer health issues and more equality in the workforce.

Getting back in the driving seat

One person in a couple losing a job can have far-reaching implications for your personal relationship. I would not suggest telling your partner, who is sitting on the couch distraught with the fact that they are out of work, 'Sure, I'll pay you'; it's more important that you understand that they feel they have lost control. They are questioning their self-worth and it's likely they are thinking, regardless of the circumstances, that this is their fault. These feelings can be even harder to deal with if they were the main breadwinner in the home and if they have never been reliant on you for money before. Think about what I just described in relation to a couple coming to a joint, mutual, voluntary decision for the benefit of the kids for one to stay at home and all the emotion that goes with that for both parties. Now remove the joint, mutual, voluntary decision part of that equation and you'll see what a horror story it is for both parties, and particularly for the person who has just lost their job.

As the person in a relationship who has not lost their job, recognising this is incredibly important. What your partner needs is very straightforward. They may not believe in themselves anymore, albeit temporarily, but it's important that you do and that you remind them of that, repeatedly, subtly and gently. This is a time when reminding them of their professional success can be useful, but only up to a point.

So be careful about what positives you focus on. For some, reminding them that this a great opportunity to spend more time with the kids will be a boost; for others it will simply remind them that they were once an airline pilot and now they are stuck at home with their already-overachieving children who were doing just great without their now-unemployed parent interrupting their lives.

Taking control of the family finances can be an empowering move. It's probably why we see many people who were in high-powered jobs, who had accumulated serious wealth until their contract ran out, contact us in our private practice. They are not sure where they are going next and they want to take on a project. They would love, once and for all, to sort out the family finances. They want to make sure everything is set up right so that if they are ever without work again they will be on top of their money and won't have to worry about it. Maybe their spouse handed them my first book and the ball started rolling from there.

One of the things I love most about these engagements is that when the couple comes in, it's regularly the person who has just lost their job who is the one in the driving seat. They are all over the finances and they know exactly what they want from the process. I'll accept that we are dealing with the upper end of the financial spectrum here, and the people I deal with in private practice have often built substantial wealth before I meet with them, but there is nothing more satisfying than going through a financial planning process with somebody in this position and showing them at the end of it all that the next job they get can pay them a third of what they were being paid before.

So, for example, you were earning €150,000 per annum, but based on your financial wealth and assuming you want to work until the age of 65, you only need to earn €50,000 per annum for the last ten years of your career. This realisation gives the individual so much power. They now know how much they need to earn in their new job and can therefore make informed decisions about what they want to do next. From time to time, when we go through this process for somebody who is out of work, we get to tell them that they have already reached financial independence; they have already reached the point in their lives where they have created enough wealth, that they don't need to work again and they don't need to worry about money. This is powerful. Now they are going back to work not because they need to but because they *want* to.

Your financial future

Whether you've been made redundant or are between jobs, knowing the date of your financial independence is incredibly advantageous. It can guide your decisions, help you make better ones and instil more value in what you're doing today because you can see the end result.

I accept that not many people who lose their job will be in this position. Most won't have the cash to get them through the next few months, never mind the rest of their lives. But there is one thing I have witnessed time and time again with people who lose their job. Within about six months they will come out with a statement, something along the lines of, 'I thought the world had come to an end, but actually losing my job was one of the best things that ever happened me professionally. I would still be there if it hadn't happened, and look at me now.'

One person in particular comes to mind. This person – let's call him John – was working on a factory floor. He had left school after his Inter Cert (Junior Cert if you're a younger reader!) and had been in this job 20 years or so when the work of the factory was outsourced to Asia and he was made redundant. John was a real grafter – worked hard, got up early – and had progressed on the factory floor. He liked what he did and had really good friends at work. John and his entire family were distraught when he lost his job.

But within six months John had a new job in sales. All of sudden he came into his own. He was out and about in his company car, meeting people, engaging with others all day. In the sales role he had more control over his financial destiny. I watched him excel in his new role, and that was partly because of his experience with briefly losing control of his finances but also because he had found something he loved doing that had the means to really provide for his family. John did so well in his new career that he soon got to go for a sales manager role. I remember asking him how the interview had gone. This guy, who had accepted and expected to spend the rest of his career on the factory floor – which is perfectly acceptable if that's what made him happy – had just given what is the best answer to an interview question I have ever heard.

He was asked: 'Give me two reasons why I should *not* give you the role of sales manager.'

John sat back and said confidently, 'Because you're stupid and you don't want to make any money.'

There was a long pause, during which John did what any good salesperson should do. He said nothing and sat staring at the country manager. The pause continued.

Then all of a sudden the country manager of this large multinational slapped the desk and said, 'Brilliant answer, just brilliant!'

It wasn't John who told me how delighted he was, with hindsight, to have lost his job. It was his wife; and she described it to me as it being not just the best thing that ever happened to John professionally, but as the best thing for the entire family. There was now significantly more money coming into the house but, more importantly, she had a happier husband. John also managed to maintain the old friendships that had been so important to him in his old job.

Trying to convince yourself – never mind somebody else – that losing your job is a good thing is very difficult without the benefit of hindsight. One thing that's much easier to accept when you're feeling lost, worried about where you're going next or how you're going to survive on social welfare is the fact that when you're out of work, professionally you're at rock bottom. You could take literally any job and be on a better wage than you currently are. You could make a decision to do anything you ever wanted to do professionally, and if you get a job doing it you'll be better off financially. You have choices and possibly for the first time in your career they are much more open than you might imagine. Realising that you're already at rock bottom is one way to ensure that in six months' time you too will be saying it was the best thing ever to happen to you.

Having these choices forced upon you is one way of triggering a professional epiphany, but having clarity of what your long-term financial future looks like can give you a similar moment, but one that you can achieve from the comfort of your current job.

That's what good financial planning is all about. It's about giving real clarity to your financial future so that you can see the long-term impact of the financial decisions you're making today. It can be a complex calculation figuring out your date of financial independence, which I'll come back to later. But try to learn from redundancy, whether it happens to you or to others – ideally getting valuable lessons from other people without ever having to go through the process yourself.

MONEY TALKS

We're not a great society here in Ireland for talking about money. In fact, one of the reasons I do what I do is because I have a core belief that people are better off if they have good financial advice. Good financial advice comes from good financial planners, advisers and journalists, but more importantly learning about money comes from each other. I accept that in private practice I can only reach a limited number of people and have positive impact on them, and this is why I started writing articles, doing things via traditional and social media, presenting a TV show and writing books. People now approach me on the street and ask me financial questions about themselves, their families, their friends. I had this happen to me recently in Dublin when a woman kept me chatting for 15–20 minutes and we discussed the finances of about seven or eight different people in her life. I love it. It feels as though the work I do has helped a country that does not talk about money to start talking about money.

In the US, they are much better at talking about money. They talk about their losses, the things that go wrong and it's almost a badge of honour: you can't succeed if at first you don't fail, is the attitude. Each failure is one step closer to a success. If you win, if things go well and you become successful in business or your career, a strange thing happens in the US: it's admired. There is no begrudgery, imagine that!

We are uncomfortable discussing money because it's instilled in us as children that we don't talk about money, that it's rude. It's like asking a lady her age. We need to change this for our kids, but also for ourselves. We need to talk about money to each other and we need to talk about money in front of our kids.

I'm not suggesting you sit your kids down and explain to them that you're struggling with the mortgage and that the family house is in danger of being repossessed; I'm talking more as a discussion between yourself and your partner as to how it's cheaper to get a takeaway than go out for dinner, but that going out for dinner is a different experience.

When you're buying a red car, you begin to see loads of red cars on the road. Similarly, once you start to really think about your finances you'll find lots of examples popping up that will help you start to discuss them with your children. Even if you don't have kids, you can still learn a lot from looking at some of the things that children should be doing early on in order to have a positive relationship with money in the future. Sometimes as adults we need to go back to basics, and there is nothing more basic than how children should be taught about money. I do regular talks with transition-year students, and I have learned so much by teaching them. I'm required to break it down to the fundamentals, bring it back to a level that is totally understandable. I have also applied the same teachings for even younger children, ones in primary school. That was difficult, but what I have found is that the way you teach things to a six-, ten- or sixteen-year-old is usually a really good way of explaining things to adults too. If you can explain something to a six-year-old in a way that they understand, you've a good chance that a 36-year-old will get it too. (A good chance, though it isn't guaranteed – there are some seriously clever six-year-olds out there!)

So, what are some of the things we can teach our kids that in turn are the things we can learn from ourselves? My kids respond really well to little games, challenges or tests when it comes to money. The smaller the nugget the bigger the impact it has on them and the more they remember. But I also like to discuss big stuff with them too – although obviously when I talk to my six-year-old about how the European Central bank uses interest rates to control inflation across the entire eurozone, I don't say it quite like that.

I might say something along the lines of, 'There's this team in Frankfurt in

Germany. It's like your football team with boys and girls on the team, but the people on the team are all really old and really boring. They have this job – do you know what they do?'

'What?'

'Their job is to make sure that the ice cream I just bought you doesn't cost way more money this time next year. So if you bought that ice cream on your birthday this year and then bought the same ice cream on your birthday next year in the same shop, it should cost a tiny bit more. But if they're deadly at their job it will cost only a little bit more. If they're crap at their job, it will cost loads more – or even worse, it will cost less.'

'But why does it cost a little more?'

'Because if the cost of the ice cream goes up a little bit it means loads of people are buying ice creams and the shop is making more money and the ice-cream maker is making more money, and it means things are going good in the world.'

Obviously when we finish the next question is often, 'What is Frankfurt?'

Explaining the role of the ECB may be a leap if it's your first venture into talking about money to your kids. But there are simpler things that are just as important – explaining that an ATM isn't a printer is a good one. You make it clear to them that at home they have their piggy bank. In it they have money and they can take their money out when they need it, but it does run out. So too does the ATM. Explain that you put your money in the bank instead of a piggy bank and they mind it for you, and when you need money there was once a time when you had to go into the bank and ask somebody to get your money out for you. Then banks decided that they would put a machine on the wall and it could give you money from your 'piggy bank' instead.

Interestingly – whether you have kids or not – when you're trying to understand something, whether it's financial or something else entirely, ask the person to explain it to you as though you are a six-year-old. It really helps them to be extremely clear. As I said, you know you have mastered a concept completely when you're able to explain something complex to someone else as though they were six years old.

This is a real challenge when you start talking about money to children: talking to them at their level. I have found this stuff really interests children – and I'm not talking about just my kids, I'm talking about any kids I meet. Try it out; look for opportunities to discuss things. When a 'money' news story comes on, take the time to try explaining things to the kids about what is going on in the world – because if they get it, you know that you get it.

Here are my top 12 money habits that anyone should be able to pass on to a child.

Twelve money habits to teach yourself (and your kids)

1. Make it fun

For years I trained young kids in GAA. Sometimes there were things you had to do: drills, skills and routines that they just didn't enjoy, like teaching them to hand-pass the ball. There are two ways you can do this. You can be methodical, technical and precise about it, or you can make it fun. The fun method produces better results. I have seen sessions where the really young kids are asked to form two lines facing each other and pick a partner and hand-pass the ball between them. The kids, who are around six, will willingly do it for a short period. But if you tell them the gap between them is lava, or a stream full of crocodiles, all of sudden the game takes on new meaning and excitement.

It's the same when it comes to competition. I know all kids are 'winners' these days, but the reality is that they love to compete. When you say to them you need to see who can keep the ball off the lava the most times or introduce some type of time clock into an activity, all of sudden the concentration levels increase and the shouts of 'Can we just play a match?' disappear.

It's the same for finance, and it's definitely the same for us adults. We need to keep ourselves interested. I never suggest keeping up with Joneses; I have spent too many years meeting the Joneses, and it's always the new client I have with the big car, the big house, the privately educated kids and all the other trapping of wealth, who turns out to be the client that most likely has a very decent salary but very little in terms of real assets when you take away all they owe from all they own. But by giving yourself your own goals, your own milestones, you can start to create a game for yourself. Nobody wants to spend hours over their finances on any day, but most of us will be happy to do a tiny bit on our finances regularly, and by doing this and seeing results, it can keep us interested. Games also need rewards – and I'll come back to this to demonstrate how reward is another important aspect to factor into your money mindset.

We are surrounded by financial education. People often ask me how I know all this stuff. It's because I'm looking for it. It's like I said about deciding to buy a red car – all of sudden you see loads of red cars on the road. If you tune yourself into learning about money, the world offers up lots of opportunity to learn – whether that's the financial news item you would once have ignored or all the different prices for milk, for example.

Open your eyes and let this stuff in, and you'll learn quickly. For your children, try to use everyday events to keep them engaged. Money is no different to any of their other learning; if you integrate it into their lives they will learn by doing. They will also spot things themselves. Talk to them about your financial reasoning for doing certain things; sometimes their simplicity helps you question your own actions. A simple one to start is the next journey you take on the roads: challenge the kids to find the cheapest petrol – or the next time you're renewing your car, home or other insurance, ask the kids to help with the online search.

Some of you reading this may not have kids, and you may not have any nieces, nephews, younger siblings or any children around you at all, but the only way we truly learn is by teaching others. As I said before, once we have grasped something well enough that we can explain it to a child in a way that they can understand, that is when we have a true understanding of that knowledge. And even if you don't have children in your life, you won't have to look very far among the adults around to find one who could benefit from being taught like a child!

Teaching kids about money is a real opportunity for both the child and the adult to learn and to benefit. Teaching 'adult children' can be equally rewarding … but can be much more demanding. When you learn something new about how to handle and improve your finances, go teach your adult mates what you learned. It will help you with your understanding and empower them to do something themselves. We don't talk about money enough, and it's time to start.

2. Learn to prioritise

Getting your first pay cheque is a big day, and for most people it's the biggest pay rise they will ever have: from zero to salary overnight. Most people never get a 100 per cent pay rise again anytime in their career. However, this can also be when the real costs kick in: rent, taxes, travel expenses and so on. If you never learned to budget when you were younger, it can be a shock to the system – especially now you've suddenly got money coming in. I've seen plenty of young workers who've committed to a high outgoing on a new car or splashed out on the fancy jacket they could never afford before, only to find that they have no money left to pay their rent at the end of the month. The lesson needed here is to differentiate between wants and needs or, to be a little blunter about it, to get your priorities right.

Let's take it back to the six-year-olds. This is around the age that a child starts to understand the concept of money and its value – although you could definitely start trying things earlier, as kids all mature at different speeds.

A great little exercise is when the child has some money and wants to buy something. Start by working it out at home; help them decide what they can and can't buy. Imagine your child has €5. They want a ball, a comic book and toy. The toy is €2, the comic book is €3 and the ball is €5. First lesson here is to convert their €5 note into five €1 coins. The important point is that they understand, if possible, that five times €1 is the same as €5.

The second lesson – and the really hard one for you to follow through on – is to ask them what they want to buy. Get them to allocate each of the coins to a toy (obviously do this at home first, not in the shop!). Your child should quickly realise that they can have the toy and the comic book, or they can just get the ball. It's important that you let them work out their own priorities. Encourage their analytical thinking by asking them to explain why they made the choice they did. But don't try and persuade them to change their mind by arguing with their rationale – that would simply be you making their decision for them. Now, this is an important part of the exercise: whatever they don't get, do *not* cave in and buy it for them. If you do, it will send the message that there is no such thing as sacrifice.

When they're ready, it's time to put everything into practice in a real shop – and you need to let your child do it for themselves. The simplest starting point for this that I witnessed was the Montessori my kids went to with their teacher 'Ali'. Each morning, Ali would bring a different child over to the shop and give them the money to pay for the milk or whatever it was they were buying. She would be with them, but they would hand over the cash and they would get the change. She also made sure they said 'thank you'.

These were pre-schoolers so there wasn't a whole pile of counting going on; it was more to do with the concept that when you take something off the shelf you don't just walk out with it – you pay with money and you say thank you. If you think about this simple thing from a child's perspective, it's powerful: kids look up to the adults around them and here they were doing an 'adult' thing and learning a valuable concept in the process.

Don't underestimate the long-term impact these exercises, simple as they are, have on children right into adulthood. While I was writing this chapter I had to attend a client meeting. I asked 'Orla', my new client, what she had learned from her parents about money. Orla is very successful in her career, and I would suggest that she is good with money. Her answer was interesting. She said that when she was a kid her mother would bring her to the supermarket to do the shopping, and when they would arrive Orla and her siblings would be given 10p each. (At that time, you could still get 10p bags. If you're reading this and are too young to remember 10p bags, they were typically a little paper bag with 10 jellies inside.) However, the task Orla and her siblings faced while their mother did the shopping was 'Should I get ten jellies, or seven jellies and one white chocolate mouse, which costs 3p?' Or the big brain conundrum was, 'Should I scrap the 10p bag completely and buy a Chomp for 10p?' Orla also got a lesson in inflation during her childhood when a Chomp suddenly went up to 12p.

Repeatedly doing exercises like this with your kids will teach them how to manage their money better; but more importantly the skills learned are transferrable to the rest of life too. They are learning how to prioritise, as well as about sacrifice and analytical thinking. But simple exercises like this are also important for us adults.

3. Focus on the reward ...

Often as adults we recognise the sacrifices: 'I didn't go out with my friends tonight because I had no money' or 'I didn't go on holidays this year because I couldn't afford it'. Let's face it, though, some of us are great at recognising what we missed out on as opposed to focusing on what we benefited from as a result of those sacrifices. If we could turn the tables on this, we could really change our relationship with money.

For example, what if we say, 'I went for dinner in my favourite restaurant on Saturday night, it was a real treat. It's expensive but it's so good. I got to do this because I didn't go for drinks after work the last two Thursdays.'

This simple change from concentrating on the reward as opposed to the sacrifice makes it feel so much better when we do make 'sacrifices'. If you think about the power of this change on small things, do it repeatedly, and then consider the long-term impact, you can become really good at it.

It's easier to focus on the rewards than the sacrifices when the reward is quite immediate. But when the reward is going to be in the medium or long term it's harder to connect the reward of the future with the sacrifice of today. Saving some of this month's wages for a house deposit, or putting money aside now into a pension so you can still afford to go out for dinner in retirement, can be a bit of a cognitive leap.

What you need to do is bring the reward back to *today*. When it comes to pensions, most pension-providers concentrate their advertising on how wonderful your life will be when you're old, should you take out one of their pensions. But they're definitely missing a trick here. I'm selfish, people are selfish; I want to know what my pension is going to do for me today. And it's actually easy to bring it back to today when it comes to the reward for putting money into a pension right now.

This is never more obvious than when I talk to large corporate groups. One of the questions I would ask the audience is, 'Who wants to pay more tax this year than they need to?'

I don't get any hands up for that one.

I then ask, 'Who is putting as much as they can afford into their pension?'

This time I may get a couple of hands.

Putting money into your pension today reduces the tax you pay today. It also means you'll provide for yourself in the future, although this is less of an incentive. As I have already said, people want a reward today.

And on that note, breaking the concept of tax down for kids is actually simpler than you might think. The next time they want a bar of chocolate, for example, open the wrapper in front of them, take a bite and hand the rest of the bar back to them. When they say, 'Hey, what did you that for?' say, 'That, little one, is tax.' It's actually the most brilliant way of us understanding tax and also explaining it to a child. You do need to elaborate and explain that you go to work and then at the end of the month your boss pays you wages, but before you get them, like with the bite out of the chocolate bar, the government takes their money from your wages to pay for things such as roads, front-line workers and even your children's school.

For you as an adult, if you want your cake and to eat it too, you can get your employer to put some of your wages directly into a pension. If you pay tax at the higher rate, it costs you €6 to invest €10 into a pension. Your take-home pay will only reduce by €6 for every €10 you put into your pension because you pay less tax. That's how tax relief on pensions work.

When it comes to other medium-term goals, such as saving for a house, it's more difficult to concentrate your thinking on the reward as opposed to the sacrifice, given that the reward is potentially three, four, five or more years away. This is why it's so important to put in short-term rewards for making progress towards long-term goals. For example, if I save consistently for three months I'll go for that weekend away, or I'll buy myself those new jeans or whatever you decide is an appropriate reward.

It's the same for kids as it is for adults; it's just their perception of what medium and long term is that differs. For example, there is zero point in asking a six-year-old to sacrifice something in May so they can go see whatever Christmas movie is going to come out in December. Instead, let them spend some money now and maybe reward them for saving something for later in the week/month/year depending on their age. 'You have €5. If you put €3 of it in the jar I'll give you €2 extra if you don't touch the jar until December.' This reward will also teach them the value of patience – something we adults often lack in the face of self-gratification.

4.   … and then get the reward

Changing your thinking to focus on the reward rather than the sacrifice is a great habit to get into, but for it to have lasting impact, the rewards do actually need to materialise. These help us to stay motivated; if it's all pain and no reward, it's unlikely that we'll stay the course. When I speak to people about saving, I always talk about having goals. But when the goal is a bigger one, which is going to take some time – such as saving for that house deposit I've mentioned – I stress the importance of short-term rewards.

Saving for a house is always difficult, and unless you win the lotto, come into money somehow or are able to tap the bank of Mam and Dad, it will take considerable time to achieve this goal. Having a goal that is a few years away can be incredibly difficult to achieve because we can lose interest and get distracted, but it's mostly because the reward is so far away that it's hard to keep on track.

This is amplified when you're in a couple, because now you're not just fighting your own lulls in motivation, you have to be conscious of your partner's lulls too. Lulls at different times to each other can make it feel like, as a couple, you're constantly lacking the motivation to keep going; you're constantly in a state where you're wondering if it's worth it. Then at other times you hit a downer about your goal together, and this is when things get risky! This is when you say, 'You know what? Let's just blow some savings on X, sure we deserve it,' and if you're both in the same state of mind at the same time, then neither of you is in a position to stop the other.

If you're saving consistently you need to recognise that you do deserve a treat from time to time, but you need to plan your treats. Agree at the outset of a long-term goal that if you save consistently for, let's say three, four or six months, then you'll reward yourselves with a weekend away, a nice meal out or something you both enjoy doing together.

Agree in advance what it is you'll do and, most importantly, when it gets to the time, do it; if you're not in a couple, decide when and what your reward will be. It can often become tempting as you approach your weekend away or meal out to cancel it because you start to wonder about the damage you're going to do to your savings. You start to wonder, *How far back is this going to push me?* or think, *But we are doing so well!* You're doing well, and you need to reward yourself for that. It won't always be easy to sacrifice things in life for some far-off distant goal, so you have to take the planned rewards.

By taking the planned rewards when you hit your little milestones it means that you don't create unplanned and often more extravagant ones on a whim. When you take the unplanned rewards, they are generally not as satisfying as the planned ones are. Yes, it is sometimes true that the best nights out with friends are the ones that happen spontaneously. But these are the exceptions to the rule. By planning something, you get three elements to your enjoyment: the anticipation, the actual experience and the memories. When the 'little reward' is part of a bigger plan, when it's because you're striving towards a bigger goal, you get an extra element: you get to feel as though you absolutely deserve it. Not just telling yourself, *Sure, I deserve this*. Really deserving it will feel so much better.

It's the opposite for the stuff you do on whim when you're trying to progress towards a bigger goal. Firstly, you lose out on the anticipation element completely. Secondly, there may be a pang of guilt as you spend your cash, and lastly, and probably most difficult of all, you can suffer 'buyer's remorse'. Yeah, we're all great at saying 'I wouldn't change a thing, it was brilliant and I would do it again tomorrow' but deep down, if we're completely frank with ourselves, we often feel guilty afterwards.

Kids are no different when it comes to needing little rewards along the way to a bigger goal. We can learn from them how we should treat ourselves. The only difference with children is that the timeframe needs to be relative. I have no idea whether this is scientific or not but it feels right, so I'll say it: time gets shorter the older you get.

I heard a great description of this at a conference in the UK once, when the speaker talked about going on a two-week holiday in the sun. You arrive the first day: it's Saturday and you're settling in, you're happy to arrive and you're starting to unwind. You relax on day one, then on day two or three you do a little exploring and identify some of the stuff you'd like to do before you go home. It's now Wednesday of your first week and you're getting your bearings, you're so relaxed you feel like you have been away for ages. Then it's your first full Saturday so you tell yourself, *I must book some of those trips*. You don't. It's now the second Saturday; you're heading home and thinking to yourself, *The second week really flew*.

I like to think of that two-week holiday as a lifespan. The first few days are your childhood, and they are the slowest. Then you arrive into your teens and early adulthood, and are thinking about your future but not really making plans. The end of week one is mid-life; you absolutely know you need to get your stuff together and plan for the future, but then all of a sudden you hit the end of the second week and your time is up. The second week of a holiday always flies. So too does the second half of life – ask anybody in their later years and they will tell you that it'll all be over in the blink of an eye.

So remember this when thinking about your own goals: what you interpret as short, medium and long term applies differently to children. They don't want and shouldn't have to think about long-term stuff. Time is relative to age, and if you want to keep them focused on the bigger goal make sure you drop little rewards along their timeline to keep them involved. And if your partner acts like a child most of the time, maybe do the same for them!

5.　Lose the negative

Both children and adults react really well to positive re-enforcement, so highlighting the benefits or rewards to financial decisions is a brilliant way to make a positive association with money. But we also need to be careful of what images we portray to our children and to ourselves.

We all know the power of positive thinking: the idea of visualising or believing in something so strongly that it comes true. 'I believe we can win the match' is a positive. Then say, 'I believe we are going to lose the match' and consider your chances of actually winning. Now think about having a conversation with yourself and reminding yourself, 'I'm broke,' or 'I'm crap with money,' or 'The money just disappears out of my account.' All of these thoughts have a negative impact on us, but can you imagine the impact it has on our kids to be around these thoughts? When children hear adults constantly saying negative things about money, they're likely to develop their own negative relationship with money.

Years ago, I had a situation myself where money was very tight. I learned a lot from it, but one of things I realised was that I was constantly talking to somebody in my life who was also having a tough time financially. We spoke to each other a lot about money and I suppose we both got comfort in the fact that there was somebody else out there in a similar position. However, this was almost like a self-fulfilling prophecy – it was becoming 'okay' to be struggling with money. I had to have a chat with the person and tell them that I couldn't talk to them about money anymore. This was a really hard thing to do. I felt like I was telling them at a time of need for them that they were on their own. But ultimately, I had to row my own boat; and I did. I genuinely believe I would not have come out of those financial struggles had it not been for the fact that I recognised that this part of my relationship with that person was having a negative impact on my own relationship with money.

I was lucky that I could continue this relationship but cut out the constant negative discussions around money. If you're having these discussions with yourself, it's harder to get away from them without consistent, conscious effort. Most damaging of all, your kids are unlikely to be able to tune out your negative comments on money; they can't not listen to the arguments you have with your partner about finances. They can't unhear you say to your partner, 'That was too expensive, it was a waste of money.' But, worst of all for kids, not only can they not turn it off, but because they look up to you, they take what you say to them as gospel.

Your attitude to money will have developed from a combination of your own experiences and what you picked up at home as a child. You can decide to change your attitude any time you want to have a more positive relationship with money. Try to imagine yourself as a child again, whether you have kids in the house or not. Now, aim to make a rule that you won't think any negative finance-related thoughts that you wouldn't want an impressionable child to pick up on. Remember that you can control what messages you send children in your life with regards to money – and that's equally important whether it's a real-life kid or your own inner child.

You're walking on thin ice in trying to develop your child's opinion about money. You need to get the balance right between never talking about money – and so creating a taboo around it so that the child feels it's something to be ashamed of – to always talking about money, which could have the child thinking about it too much and becoming obsessive about it. We all have that one mate who is mad about money, always talking about it, always wanting to know how much people earn and how much things cost. Next time you're chatting to that person, subtly try and check out whether their parents talk about money all the time. You might be surprised.

The way we discuss money around children has subtle but long-lasting impacts on their attitude towards it. But everything applies to you, too. The way you talk to yourself about money, the way you discuss it with others, what others say, how much or how little it's talked about, how positive or negative you or the people around you are about money; all of this has an impact on your attitude towards it. Try to start blocking out what isn't helping and let in what is. Once you control the narrative, you're taking control of your money and your money is no longer controlling you. Just remember that changing a lifetime's thoughts on money can take time and patience – something we adults often lack.

6. Be patient

In the world we live in, immediate gratification is plentiful. We scroll through Twitter at a rate of knots, absorbing data in succinct paragraphs. Instagram is even quicker with the pictures, videos and data; and then TikTok brings things to a whole new level with 60-second videos. It gives new meaning to the Mark Twain quote, 'If I had more time, I would have written you a shorter letter.' To be successful on these platforms, people have to sum up what they are trying to say; and they must do it in an entertaining and informative way.

We need little concentration and so the 'hit' is immediate. But it's not just about the content. It's how easily information moves from one person to another! No need to wait for the postman to receive your letter: *You've got mail*. You don't even need to arrange to visit your loved ones: video-calling, particularly during the pandemic, is now the norm, even for the older generations.

When we can transport ourselves across the world like Mike Teavee in *Charlie and the Chocolate Factory*; order a movie without leaving our couch; have our shopping delivered to our door; our dinner cooked by somebody else and a driver arriving with it within minutes; and can do all of that via the Internet on our phones, I think it's fair to say we have reached a realm of instant satisfaction of all our needs that we could never have previously imagined.

Is it any wonder, then, that compared to previous generations we are happy to borrow money to buy cars, holidays or even a restaurant meal? We stick it on the credit card because we know what we want and we want it *now*. But why is it important to have patience in our financial dealings?

Teaching patience with money really flushes out our impulses to buy stuff we don't actually need. It allows us to make much better and informed decisions about what we want. As the days pass, our needs and wants change and we can often totally change direction about what we want to spend our money on. And, more importantly, we can become attached to our savings.

I see it all the time. Adults in their mid-twenties or later find themselves in a position where they have savings for the first time. It may have accumulated during a Covid lockdown or some other event. These people become not only attached to their savings, but they also become addicted to the routine of saving. Ask somebody in this position to use that money to pay for something big that is going to put a serious dent in their savings and it can result in some peculiar reactions. People who previously would have whacked it on the credit card and got that instant hit now sit back and wonder whether they really want this item or not.

But this can go too far. Some people get so attached to their savings that they do something even more incredible: they consider not using their savings, but instead borrowing money to satisfy their instant gratification requirements. In very basic terms you're walking into your bank, lodging your hard-earned savings at one account and they are agreeing to pay you little or no interest for the pleasure of them having full use of your money. You say thank you, you walk away from that counter and over to another counter and fill out a form to borrow your own money from the same bank and in return they charge you 6, 8 or 10 per cent and more in interest for giving you a loan *of your own money*.

Think about the maths on this. If you have €10,000 in savings with a bank and you managed to get 0.5 per cent interest on it for five years, ignoring tax in five years' time, your €10,000 will be worth €10,252. Now if you borrow €10,000 at 8 per cent over five years the repayments will be €202.76 per month. This means you'll make total repayments of €12,165 over the next five years. The difference between the two is €1,913. In other words, the bank will have made €1,913 by lending you your own money. Why? Because you wanted instant gratification and had become attached to your savings.

It is often – though not always – instant gratification that drives us to borrow money. There is the rare occasion when there is an actual emergency and we *need* to borrow money, but more frequently it's to do something like buy a new car or go on holiday.

The right thing to do is to save up for these expenses, but because we want them now, because we want instant gratification, we come up with all sorts of behavioural biases to reaffirm to ourselves as to why we need a new car. 'I had a second-hand one before and it always broke down, never again,' for example, or 'Sure isn't the PCP great value?' Or the best one: 'It's 0 per cent finance.' Really? You don't think the interest isn't hidden in the sticker price of the car?

A car is a great example of our need for instant gratification. The new-car smell doesn't last that long, yet we keep going back, over and over, and buying new motors. My mate recently bought a brand-new car. It was stunning: sleek black, coupé, it had the works on it and was a cracking car. A few weeks after he got it, though, he said to me, 'You know what, Eoin? Now it's just my car.'

I may have caught him during a moment of buyer's remorse, but the point really struck me. I know we can talk all we want about how the value of a car drops once we drive it off the forecourt. We all know this. But the opposite to instant gratification is also what happens when we buy a new car. Even though we know it has just dropped in value we also know – or at least we tell ourselves – that we won't be selling it for ages, so it doesn't matter. We all want the reward now and the pain later – but recognising that this usually isn't the best way of purchasing something is an immeasurably important lesson.

Because reality check: new cars are an expensive mistake. If you like a 'newish' car then the optimum time to buy is when the car is two years old. Depreciation is most dramatic in the early years. Obviously it depends on the make, model, mileage and condition of the car, but it also depends on other factors such as supply and new models being released. I have seen suggestions that cars depreciate by numbers varying from 20 per cent to 70 per cent in the first two years. But let's take it as being closer to the lower end of the scale. Let's assume 30 per cent. That means a car costing €30,000 new will cost €21,000 when it's two years old. Why not let somebody else take that €9,000 hit instead of you? Whether it's new or used, the car will still smell the same two weeks after you leave the garage anyway.

Now let's return to our six-year-olds. If adults are already at the stage of needing immediate and instant gratification, what hope have our children got? When I was younger, it was pretty standard to have to wait a little bit longer for the things I wanted. For example, the 28 days I had to wait for my Dinky car to arrive after I had collected and sent off the tokens from the back of the Rice Krispies packet made me love that car even more. When I consider how instant things are for the next generation, I worry.

Many have never even experienced a world when they had to wait until next week for a new episode of a TV series. In fact, most don't even watch 'linear TV' anymore. When I go into a secondary school I explain to students what linear TV is. I say, 'Linear TV is a TV station that is broadcasting the same programmes into all houses at the same time, for example RTÉ, BBC or Channel 4. Linear TV is not Netflix or YouTube. With those platforms you decide what is being broadcast to you at any given time.'

Once they get the concept, I ask them, 'Put your hand up if you have watched linear TV in the last seven days.'

Typically about 10–15 per cent of the room will put their hand up. I then say, 'Put your hand down if the linear TV you watched was live sport.'

I usually end up with 5 per cent or less of the room with their hand still in the air.

I accept that this is not a scientific poll, but the results are so consistent from school to school and location to location around the country that I feel the numbers are not far off. Based on my experience it means that less than 5 per cent of our 16-ish year olds are watching linear TV on a regular basis (not great for me as a linear TV presenter!).

This means they are consuming their content from places like Netflix or YouTube – where they are getting the content they want instantly, but they are also not getting the content they *don't* want. When they don't like something, when they stop a video early because they are not getting instant gratification from it, they move to the next video. The platform provider learns from what they like and what they don't like and adjusts the algorithm based on their previous behaviour. This results in more 'interesting' content being shown to them to keep them hooked on YouTube, Netflix or whatever it is they are watching.

This instant gratification is smart technology working as it should – but it does result in users not feeling fulfilled if they don't get the same instant gratification from other things. Streaming content is just one example, but this also applies to other things like online gaming, to needing a lift everywhere instead of walking and even down to what our children eat.

I often speak about the 72-hour rule. This rule states that if you want something, don't buy it now, put it back and wait 72 hours. If you still want it then maybe, just maybe, it's something you should buy. It's an excellent practice for adults to get into, but you can also think about trying this with your kids: it will mean that they only buy stuff they actually want, but it will also teach them that good things take time. If you teach them the discipline to save up for something, you're teaching them a life-long lesson. It's tempting when a child saves for a little while for something for you to 'top them up' to get them over the line. Don't.

If you let them do it themselves, it can be interesting to see what happens next. When your kid has managed to save all the money that they needed for that one thing they wanted, it's not unusual for them to reassess the situation. All of sudden this money, which was hard got and took a long time to save, is about to be gone. This is gold, because you have taught them patience. They are now questioning whether the thing they are about to buy is more valuable than the attachment they now have to their savings.

7.   Let go of your emotions

We could all do ourselves a favour if we removed any emotional attachment we sometimes place on our loans. The most blindingly obvious situation I see this happening in is with weddings. A couple falls madly in love, they are getting on with life and then decide to get married. Financially they may not be fully prepared for it but 'we only plan on getting married once'. 'I want the day to be perfect' and 'I have such a big family, they all need to be there.' People convince themselves that their cousin Johnny needs to be at the wedding, and it's only after the invites go out that they are told sure Johnny has been living in Australia for the past two years.

After the wedding is done and all the cash gifts are spent lots of couples are left with the wedding loan. They borrowed money from the bank or credit union and now three years later it's still coming out of their bank account every month and in some cases is hampering their ability to get a mortgage.

Of all the loans people take out during their lives it's the wedding loan that they are most defensive about. The wedding loan is, in my opinion, the ultimate 'forget about patience, reward now, regret later' loan. But the regret bit is so hard for couples to stomach. When I question couples about their feelings around their wedding loan and I ask them whether they wish they didn't have the loan, they usually assure me that they wouldn't change a thing.

Resenting a wedding loan, particularly when the loan is holding you back financially, doesn't mean you hate your wedding day. It doesn't mean you made the wrong choice in life partner. It doesn't mean you failed, or that you made any type of mistake. It's a loan. It's okay to hate it. In fact if you don't hate your debt you'll be happy for it to hang around. If you do hate it, you'll try to get it out of your life. *We need to dissociate the loan from the thing we used the loan for.* The wedding is a great example of finances being tied up inextricably with emotions.

It's the same with all loans. You can like your car but hate your car loan. You can love your new clothes and hate your credit card debt. We need to stop letting ourselves off the hook with 'I wouldn't change a thing' or 'but I love it/him/her'. The things we have in our life are not actually connected to how we pay for them and until we break that psychological connection we will continue to seek that instant gratification and continue on our journey of borrowing from the future to pay for today. By disconnecting the money from the thing that was bought with it, we can make more rational decisions in terms of dealing with that debt.

We've already talked about how we either become exactly the same as or exactly the opposite of our parents when it comes to money. What is clear is that people who resent debt had parents who were strongly against borrowing or who borrowed recklessly and continuously. I can't think of a single client who really resented borrowing who had a parent in the middle, a parent who borrowed from time to time and was never under pressure from financial debt.

I have never seen somebody successfully get out of troublesome debt without first resenting that debt. To clear up an issue with debt you first need to reach the point where you absolutely hate it. It needs to be consuming you to the point where you just want it gone. If you reach that point and then successfully clear it, you won't get into that state again. I have seen people who have cleared significant debt but unfortunately for them the debt had not yet become so troublesome for them that they hated it. When this happens it worries me, because I know it's only a matter of time before they rebuild their debt issue and maybe next time is when they get to breaking point and start to hate it. But the worst situation of all is when you never reach the point of hatred and you spend your entire life in a debt cycle that is never quite bad enough to put you under on any given day but silently kills your financial future. Until one day you wake up and it's Wednesday of the second week of your holiday and you realise you have no cash to get you through until you leave on Saturday.

Interestingly the people I see most affected in this way are people who earn really good money. Somebody who earns €300,000 or €400,000+ a year can get personal loans, car loans and credit cards really easily and so the spiral is much easier to feed. They do this to the detriment of long-term financial planning and in the strong belief that the income will last forever. It doesn't. I have had countless client discussions with people who wake up in their mid-to-late-fifties, they earn really good money, they are often professional and right now are at the peak of their career. I'm talking about barristers, doctors, consultants. From the outside they have the amazing house, brand-new, expensive car, privately educated children and they enjoy their big holidays every year. They work so hard the finances take a back seat. They work so hard they feel, probably quite rightly, that they 'deserve' all the trappings with which they surround themselves.

They earn such good money that two things happen. The first is that they lure themselves into a false sense of believing the money will never come to an end. They forget that one day their hands, their brain or their body will mean they will have to stop working. This means they never really think properly about themselves in the future. Don't get me wrong, I'm not saying this is the same for all professionals earning good money, but it is for some. The second thing that happens is that they are offered easy access to money. They can get their hands on credit cards and the credit-card companies throw money at them. 'You want a €5,000 limit, doc? Here, have €20,000 just in case – sure, you don't have to use it.'

When these clients first engage with me, they have reached a critical point. They are realising that the end of the career runway is in sight and they are hoping they haven't left it too late. They may have a few properties that have been remortgaged a few times to pay for the lifestyle. They are subsidising the rent they are getting on their properties to meet the mortgage repayments and they are realising that what was once bought as their 'pension' is still costing them money as they reach pensionable age.

But no different than the newlyweds, you ask them about the things they have spent the money on and they can become quite defensive. 'I work hard, I need to live too' or 'I like my cars' or 'we go to the Maldives every year, it helps me recharge and come back refreshed, I have no doubt it pays for itself in terms of my productivity when I come back'. Again, they connect the loans with the event, experience or thing. Having a holiday does not mean you have to have a loan. But if you did take one out, hating your loan does not mean you hated your holiday.

As a parent, if you want to teach your kids to hate debt then either let them see you hate yours or instil the old-school 'Never borrow for something – if you can't pay for it you can't afford it.' It's the same with yourself. Make a decision today to hate your debt. Realise that for every €1,000 you leave on your credit card for a year, in simple interest terms it's probably costing you €200. This is an expensive way for you to live and a great way for the banker to pay for their own holiday.

I've never seen anybody successfully tackling a serious debt issue without first hating the loans. They need to hit absolute rock bottom. It's just before this point that I worry most about clients in serious debt. They are ready to crack. They are engaging with the banks, doing what they can. They move their money around, robbing Peter to pay Paul, trying to keep everyone else happy while they get more and more miserable until they reach a point where they say they can do no more. *I'm doing my best. Let them come at me because actually I hate the situation I'm in. I hate that I can't see a way out and I hate my debt.* Eureka.

From this point on I see clients change. They engage with their debt, they come to agreements about payment plans and they accept it took a long time to accumulate the debt and it's going to take a long time to get rid of it. It's going to be hard, they accept that. They know stuff in their lives will need to change to get rid of this debt and they resent the debt because of that. It often resembles a weighing scales. The more they hate their debt the more positive they become about clearing it. They know every cent they pay off the debt is getting rid of one little bit of something they hate.

If they never reach that point of misery and they manage to bring themselves back from the edge, inevitably they will end up back in debt again. They never fell out with their debt so they are happy to welcome it back into their lives. A perfect example of all this was a phone call I had with a prospective client. On paper they looked like the type of client we often deal with in the practice. They had told us in advance they were earning €400,000+, they had considerable property assets and owned two businesses. When I got on the phone to them, they then told me about their debt. They were absolutely swamped and wanted our help to clear down all their debt and start funding a pension for retirement for the first time. This prospective client was 57. They started to list off all the debts they wanted to clear. I asked if they had a credit card. They said they did but they were going to leave that alone because it had a €20,000 limit and it was handy to have, and they currently had €14,000 on the card.

There are two reasons we didn't take on this client: the first because it's not the type of work we do in private practice; the second because it was obvious that whoever took on that case, unless they could get the client to the point where they never wanted to see a loan again, never mind a credit card, any plan they came up with would be doomed to failure. This person did not see their debt as being the issue. They just felt they had plenty of income and it was just about coming up with the right plan to sort it out. The problem was that this person had not addressed the root cause of why the borrowing happened in the first place, and therefore a plan that was starting to make progress would immediately be knocked back ten steps when the credit card got maxed out and the client's friendly banker rang them offering yet another personal loan. They hadn't reached the point where they never wanted to get into debt again and so they never would address their debt problem.

Breaking any excuse you have given yourself for having debt is the only way to get rid of the problem of debt for good. To get out of debt and stay out of it you need to hate it. I have seen people who are happy to go off and borrow money for lots of things they never wanted, never mind needed. I have never seen somebody get into serious debt who 'hates borrowing' – these people learned to hate debt from an early age. Most likely it was instilled or motivated by their parents' behaviour. They were the lucky ones who learned from others to hate their debt as opposed to having to learn themselves.

And it's actually quite easy to do this. Teaching kids that debt is a bad thing is one of the most important pieces of financial wisdom you could ever pass to them. Try to do it in simple ways. Yep, it might hurt you and them when they borrow money from you that you actually charge them interest, but it's better to learn about interest in your sitting room and with their pocket money than it is in a luxury German car dealership.

8. Think like a banker

Teaching yourself to hate debt is a valuable lesson to learn – but don't underestimate the power of the opposite, either. Debt cripples us because somebody else is making money off our need to reward ourselves instantly. Coming to terms with the other side of the debt is a twofold lesson. The first part is that money can make you money, but the second part is that giving out money is risky.

Regardless of the terms and conditions, it's inevitable that at some point in our lives we will need to borrow money. When buying a house, most people will need to get a mortgage or at the very least a decent loan from somewhere like a credit union.

I was recently doing a talk to transition-year students in my own secondary school. At 'little break' I had a surreal experience. I was brought to the staff room for coffee. I spent five years in that school and never once saw the inside of the staff room. At the time it had been about 20 years since I had left the school. Looking around the staff room there were lots of new, young-looking teachers sitting around chatting, but I was also surprised to see some of the same teachers who had taught me, albeit with a bit more 'experience' etched on their faces. I got speaking to one of my old teachers who expressed to me how great it was that I was in teaching transition-year students about money and how they wished that when they were that age somebody had done the same with them. They then went on to tell me that when they were 27 years old they had a life-changing chat with somebody who 'knew about money'.

In this chat, they had told their friend that they were saving really hard for a house. The friend asked had they applied for a mortgage yet and the teacher asked, 'What's a mortgage?' This teacher had never heard of a mortgage and didn't even know that banks gave out loans to help people buy a house. They were saving all the money needed to buy a house and they were 'nearly there'.

The teacher in question was saving for a house in the mid-90s. To put this feat in perspective, in 1995 the average house price in Ireland was just over €76,000 and although I don't know what this teacher was earning at that particular time the average wage in Ireland in 1995 was €17,873. He needed to save 4.3 years of gross income to be able to afford the average house. Allowing for tax and substantial and regular savings he would probably need to save for ten years to get there. He was 27 and was 'nearly there'.

My initial reaction to this was that this was absolute madness: he was trying to *save* for a house, a whole one! But he was actually doing things, albeit through naivety, the right way around. A quick google will tell you that there is a cohort of people who think the mortgage was only designed to allow bankers to make money. Let me be clear: bankers do make money off mortgages and that is why they were invented. However, these theorists suggest that society is forced into believing we need to own property and without it we have no security. They believe this has been forced on us because banks have money sitting in their bank accounts that they want to make money off. They wanted to make money on things that were safe so they created a societal demand (all by themselves!) for property so they could lend people money on the strength of these properties. If the person did not pay the money back they could take the property back and society would still value the property and they could sell it on to somebody else who would most likely need a mortgage to buy it and so the cycle continues.

This sounds very plausible because it's more or less true; it's all quite accurate – except for the fact that the theorists are giving a ridiculous amount of credit to the bankers. I struggle to believe they have that much impact on society, having themselves an engrained requirement to own property. People like owning houses and cars and shoes and paintings. It's true we often buy things because of what these things tell others about who we are – but we choose to buy them. Society has brought us to this point and the banks have simply hopped on the band wagon.

As adults, we need to accept that banks don't work for us: they work for themselves. What the banker gets from their interaction with you is their salary. We go into lots of things in life knowing and understanding the commercial realities of what we are going into. When we walk into a restaurant, we know that we will (hopefully) enjoy a nice atmosphere, a comfy chair, good service and delicious food, and in return we will pay a fair price for that. It's clear and transparent – we are getting what we paid for. Some of us, however, have a more clouded perception of what banks are there for. We think they're there for societal good, to 'help' us get our house. They're not. They're there to make money, and in the process of them making money they may well sell you something like a mortgage, which 'helps' you to buy your home.

So many people are paying a little more for their mortgage because 'the bank have always been good to me'. This is branding. The definition of branding is where you can convince somebody to pay a little more money for something that they could get of a similar quality elsewhere because they associate your company with a brand. Apple is a master at this – millions of people pay more for Apple products they could get of similar quality elsewhere because they are *Apple* products. XYC bank should not garner this same support. Banks are a utility provider – that's it. The sooner we realise they are there to make money off us, the sooner we will start to improve how we approach, interact and engage with them. The next time you have to engage with a bank for whatever reason, remember you're the customer. Banks need customers to keep the lights on but if they think you're going to be hassle they won't take you on, so present yourself in the best possible light. If you do this, then as a customer you'll always have your pick of the banks.

Getting children to think dynamically about both sides of the borrowing equation is useful when it comes to them understanding how a banker's mind works. It's a very common situation for me to be talking to somebody who just can't understand why they can't get a mortgage or a loan for their new car. There's often something glaringly obvious why they are not attractive to a lender. When I finally say something like 'you would need to use 90 per cent of your income to meet the mortgage repayments each month' people tend to get the message very quickly.

Getting a holistic view of how lending money out and borrowing money works is a life lesson that both adults and children can benefit from. If you have more than one child, consider encouraging them to lend money among themselves. It's an easy operation to set up; as a parent or guardian you generally know which of your children still has their birthday money and which child lets money burn a hole in their pocket. When the child who can't keep money for longer than 20 minutes comes looking for money off you, don't give it to them. Instead send them to the sibling who is loaded. It's important to realise that just like a central bank your role in all of this is to supervise but not to interfere. Let them decide their own terms: is there interest or will the borrower have to do jobs around the house for the other instead of interest? What security is being requested or being offered? It's really interesting to see if the person giving out the money considers all the eventualities and outcomes. If they don't the first time and it all goes wrong, I can assure you they will protect themselves if ever they dream of going into a similar deal again.

Once the commercial terms are decided then let them at it, and whatever you do don't bail the broke child out if it all goes pear-shaped. This is a terrible lesson for both parties to get, that the 'supervisor' steps in and sorts everything out at their own cost – 2008 anyone?

I used to do this with my teenage son and daughter when they were younger. One of them was good at holding on to their money and the other would literally have borrowed their birthday money weeks if not months in advance of their big day. This meant arriving at their birthday hoping that the birthday cards contained more cash than they owed out, or at very least the same amount of cash so that they didn't end up a year older and even more broke.

The deals were often fascinating to watch. I recall one that took place in the car as we were driving to town to go shopping. I won't embarrass them by naming them! Child 1 had a gift voucher for a shop, and they offered to sell it to child 2. Child 1 needed cash and the voucher was not something they could use immediately. The voucher was for €50. Child 2 didn't need the voucher right away either but it was for a shop they always buy stuff in and they had plenty of savings so they saw a great opportunity. Child 2 said they would buy the €50 voucher for €40.

Initially child 1 was absolutely horrified and refused point blank. Then child 2 started to drop little nuggets or enticements: 'We won't be in town again for ages, maybe your top won't be there next time!'

The brilliance/deviousness came next though. Child 1 said, 'Give me €45 and I'll sell it to you.'

Child 2 immediately dropped their offer to €35. Child 1 offered the €40 and child 2 accepted.

The deal was done and the money and voucher exchanged hands. It was at this point where my moral dilemma hit me hard and I had a crossover of professional admiration and trying to be a good dad because child 2 said, 'Dad, I've checked online, the shoes you're going in here to buy are available in the shop the voucher is for. Do you want to buy a €50 voucher for €45?'

That was a proud moment for a financial-planner dad to watch. But I was really stuck to know what to do. Child 1 was jumping up and down with disgust and trying to reverse the deal by grabbing the voucher and throwing the cash back.

As the 'supervisor' in this instance I immediately stepped in and stopped the physical element of the interaction. I explained the deal was done and both parties agreeing to their deal remained valid. Still, to this day I wonder was my next move the right one or not. I thought about the offer on the table to me. I was getting a 10 per cent discount on a €50 voucher I was going to use in the next 20 minutes anyway. It would be silly for me to not use it. I also admired child 2 for their ability to know their audience, carry out the required research and execute the deal while keeping their mouth shut. But I did feel for child 1 who had effectively been caught out. In the end, I bought the voucher: child 1 learned a valuable lesson, child 2 honed their deal-execution skills and I got a fiver off my shoes.

These deals are something my kids love doing. They also involved one child (always child 2) lending money to the other (always child 1). As they progress, the T&Cs change: they charge more interest and they get chores done or favours. It encourages enterprising behaviour, but it's always so tempting to stop being the financial planner and do my real job, which is to be a dad. Child 1 often feels hard done by when the T&Cs being offered are out-and-out unfair, but my response is always one of two: either you didn't have to accept the deal or you accepted the deal and now you must live with it.

A bit like every other company out there selling anything, banks have found a way to make money off what society believes and what society wants. In the same way, my child 2 has learned how to make money and get chores done off my child 1. Child 2 sees an opportunity in child 1's needs and is, let's be fair, exploiting it. I do question my moral judgement on these interactions, but on balance I believe that the lessons they learn are valuable. And although it's painful for them, I would much prefer my kids to be learning from each other when the stakes are low than later on with higher consequences and some banker cashing in on them.

9. Borrow from yourself

It's always incredible to me how somebody – let's call them Sam – can walk into a bank and give their savings to the teller to put in a savings account. They accept the bank will pay them probably less than 0.10 per cent interest per year before tax. Once Sam has finished depositing their hard-earned savings they make another decision. They decide that before they leave the bank, they will go over to the lending desk and enquire about a loan. The lending clerk punches a few numbers into the computer and agrees to lend Sam some money at an interest rate of 8 per cent.

Now let us assume that Sam put €10,000 into savings and just happened to borrow €10,000 from the same bank. Basically, what has happened is Sam gave the bank their own money and then the bank lent it back to them at a considerably higher interest rate than the rate the bank gave to Sam for their savings. Sam has been charged for getting a loan of their own money.

You might point out that Sam still has their savings, but it's still a nonsensical argument. You see, not dissimilarly to how we feel about loans, we often become emotionally attached to our savings. Why wouldn't we? We work hard and saving it is difficult, so we can become quite protective over our savings. But more importantly than the fact that savings can be hard to come by is that they also offer us something extra: a financial security blanket. Some people sleep better at night because they have savings. For others, the idea of dipping into their savings when they could get a loan instead is just something they wouldn't do. These people are often serial borrowers and often take out one loan to replace and top up another one.

Sam's example makes it very clear how crazy it is. Sam literally walks into the bank with their cash and walks out with their own cash, which has been filtered through the banking system – and are being charged a hefty spread for the pleasure. Sometimes it's harder to see the less obvious example of the very same thing. For example, having money with one bank or credit union and then getting a loan from a different institution doesn't feel quite the same as Sam's situation. Nor does simply having savings and a loan at the same time. Maybe you have had the loan for ages and you've only recently accumulated the savings. Now you might be wondering should you clear the loan.

It's only by decoupling our emotional attachment to our savings that we can then make the right logical decisions about how best to use them. Should you use savings instead of getting a loan or should you use savings to clear an existing loan?

At its most basic level it's quite easy to figure this out, because it's simple maths. Most investments pay tax on the growth at a rate of 41 per cent. Allowing for taxes and a bit of fat for yourself I would suggest that if you can get an interest rate of double the interest rate of your loan then it makes sense to clear off a loan. For example, if you have a loan at an interest rate of 8 per cent then you would need to get 16 per cent growth on your savings for it to make sense to invest rather than to clear the loan. Now getting 16 per cent growth consistently on an investment is an absolute hope and not an expectation. When you start to think about loans on credit cards at 22 per cent you would need to get 44 per cent growth for it to make financial sense to keep your cash and not to clear the loan, never mind the massive 86 per cent growth you would need to get on your online clothes-shop account that you're not clearing in full each month.

But at the other extreme, if you have a tracker rate of 1 per cent it's reasonable to assume that if you pick the right long-term investment you could expect to get 2 per cent plus before tax per annum from it over the long term. Therefore it does not make sense to clear the loan.

Obviously I'm simplifying this and there are other factors you could bring into this. For example, if you're a higher-rate tax payer you could put your savings into your pension, which means you get an even bigger bang for your buck. If a higher-rate tax payer puts €10,000 into a pension they will pay €4,000 less in tax. In other words, it costs €6,000 to put €10,000 into a pension. Turning

€6,000 into €10,000 is 66 per cent growth and that is before you even invest the money. (A standard-rate tax payer gets 25 per cent uplift since it costs them €8,000 to get €10,000 into a pension.) This is why it's always so frustrating for me when I come across people who pay extra off their mortgage each month but don't actually maximise their pensions contributions. These people are making their financial lives much more complicated than they need to be.

Of course, the maths makes it seem simple, but life sometimes isn't that simple. We all know life isn't linear. There are times when holding on to your savings is the right thing to do even if the loan is very expensive. For example, if you're going to wipe out your savings to clear a loan then it raises a flag of concern: because no sooner do you press the button on this than the car needs to be replaced or the washing machine breaks down or some other event happens where you need ready access to your money. When you do need to borrow, particularly in an emergency, you're likely to try and get a new loan as quickly as possible.

And the easier it is to borrow money the more expensive the interest rate. We see this with mortgages; you're made to jump through hoops with lots of documentation and forms and your mortgage is likely to be the cheapest money you'll ever borrow. Yet something like a credit card is approved quickly, yet every time you use it you're literally borrowing money. It's easy. And it's expensive. You use your all savings to clear your 8 per cent personal loan, life happens and you put money on the credit card at 20 per cent plus. You have replaced a cheaper loan with a more expensive one and the banker wins again.

Kids are not out borrowing money and weighing up the interest rates versus the projected investment returns available or calculating how much tax relief is available to them, but the lesson they need to learn about this is exactly the same one we need to teach ourselves as adults. We should all see money for what it is. It's not status, it's not a representation of achievement, it's simply a tool to be used to buy things that make our lives liveable, comfortable and enjoyable. Sometimes its goal is to leave you sleeping soundly at night, and the financial security you get from having some savings does that. But other times we have irrational, emotional attachments to our savings. Money can consume us and having any sort of emotional attachment to it often leads us down the path of making the wrong decisions with it.

I know people who pay interest on a €2,000 credit-card balance each month but yet have €20,000 in savings because they 'don't want to touch their savings'. They simply can't see the wood for the trees. You need to connect the dots of all your finances. Compartmentalisation can be useful in some situations but not when it comes to long-term financial strategy. For this to work, you need to analyse each individual part of your finances and then bring it all together to come up with the financial plan.

I have this discussion with new clients all the time. Sometimes people come to my private practice and when they are first engaging over the phone, they say things like, 'I don't want to look at everything, I just want to get advice on what to do with the X amount of money I have sitting in my bank account.' This is a bit like going to your GP and asking them to fix your sore knee. You then leave without telling them your two elbows and other knee are also sore. Your finances, like your body, are all joined together. We need to make sure we consider them holistically.

This is really difficult balancing act because I'm now going to sound like I'm totally contradicting myself when I say there are times when we need to be emotionally invested in our money. For example, you should name your savings. If your savings are called 'rainy-day fund' it justifies dipping into them for some splurge expenditure because it's an emotionally rainy day. If you call your savings pot 'weekend away in August' and you have a bad day, then you're less likely to raid your trip-away fund.

We need to be invested in our money, we need to feel it's of value to us or we will squander it, but we can only allow ourselves this emotional attachment in compartments. You need to hate your debt and love your savings; you also need to name your savings in order to create this emotional attachment. But it's when you get to the strategy level and you're taking a more long-term view of all of your different financial compartments that you need to try and remove the emotion. This will allow you make better long-term financial decisions.

People often say to me when I'm giving advice that they think it all seems so straightforward, that there's nothing overly complex in what I'm recommending, yet they're scratching their heads wondering why they didn't come up with the plan. The reason is that although they may be doing the *right things*, I don't think they are doing *things right* – and there is a huge difference. I have the advantage of having no emotional attachment to any of the savings or loans in front of me. I'm simply looking at a client's long-term finances, seeing where I want them to end up and working back from there.

It's about recognising our different pots of savings and understanding that sometimes our savings could be working harder for us than they currently are. If you can clear a loan and still have decent savings left over then it's likely that is the right thing to do. So do it. But be careful what you do next. If you have been meeting the loan repayments, you now need to make sure you allocate those loan repayments to something else rather than allowing lifestyle creep. Otherwise you'll find that a few months later you have no loan, a big dent in your savings and you still feel like you have no extra money in your pocket.

If you use your savings to clear a loan, then your savings need to be paid back. Equally, if you decide to use your savings instead of getting a loan then you need to work out what the loan would have cost you and pay your savings back at that rate per month. Banks make money from the interest they charge you. Next time you need to borrow money, see if you can borrow it from yourself. Can you borrow the money from your own savings and pay it back the same way you would a bank loan? Pay for your own holiday, not your banker's holiday.

As for how this can be taught to a child, it's fairly straightforward. The next time your kid has money, encourage them to compartmentalise by breaking it into different pots. Get them to name each pot after what they are going to use it for. If they have physical cash, get them to physically divide up the pots on the table in front of them. When they have it broken down with €2 here, €3 there, etc. bring their attention to the entire table and ask them to think what they could do if they used all the money at the same time just for one thing. Your aim is for them to be able to grasp the concept of the pots while also seeing the bigger picture of all the money in front of them.

10. Do deals

I remember when I went Kusadasi in Turkey; I think it was around 1996 and I went for two weeks with my dad and his long-time pal for a lads' holiday. I was a teenager, they weren't. Any of you who have followed me will know how much of an influence my dad has been on me and with this holiday I observed him do something repeatedly that made me realise, *I'm really crap at that.*

At the time – and I assume still to this day – Kusadasi was full of street traders, stalls and shops that spilled out on to the streets. The environment was buzzing. I recall one shop was called 'Michael Baldwin' after the character in *Coronation Street* and the guy who ran it was a brilliant salesman. The clothes he was selling looked really well, seemed to be of reasonable quality and carried the logos of all the top brands (although I doubt Ralph Lauren ever made a penny from the sale of these particular shirts).

What I learned from my observations was my dad's ability to haggle. I hated haggling then and hate it now. Some people have a real skill for this and my dad was one of those people. He would start by building a relationship, getting to know the guy, completely ignoring his initial offers and totally changing the subject when he made them. He would then express a passing interest in something and allow the suggested price to come at him. Whatever the price, Dad would always laugh at it and put the item down again. Then the haggling would start – Dad would offer something ridiculous and we would all hear about the kids the trader had to feed.

But the real skill in all of this was Dad's ability to know exactly when to walk away. He would get the trader to invest enough of his time, he would dangle the sale in front of him for long enough and then he would turn on his heels and walk off with the trader following him down the street, counteroffering. It didn't always work, but more often than not Dad would get a price many people would fail to achieve.

I learned something really important on the streets of Kusadasi that I still use to this day: you have to be willing to walk away. I mean, really willing. For example, if you're bidding on a house, you need to decide before you get into the bidding war what your limit is. Decide it before you get caught up in the emotion. If you're in a couple, make sure you decide together at what price you're both willing to walk away without any regret. When you reach that price you need to accept that it was never meant to be and move on. I have seen people do this only to find later that the auctioneer or estate agent – like the street trader – comes back afterwards because the other bidder fell through. Or they lose the house and find something else entirely. Whatever the outcome, if you can make a decision in advance and stick to it you're making a decision based on finances and not emotions.

Decide, dive, drip

When it comes to bidding on houses, it's an emotional time. Strip the emotion out of the process by applying the three Ds: decide, dive, drip.

Decide – know where you're going to stop before you even start. Pick a price that is your absolute limit. Don't choose a round number because then you'll always be asking yourself whether you should have gone a bit higher. Instead of picking €300,000, pick €300,500. Be sure you and your partner – if you have one – totally agree that this is all the house is worth to you; and do this before you put the first bid in, because once that first bid goes in and the counterbids start coming you're going to see this emotional, irrational demon coming out of your partner – or out of you if you're bidding on your own.

Dive – when you know what your limit is, start well below it. Estate agents are required to pass your bid on; don't insult anybody but don't go too close to your limit to begin with. Get the balance right: no different to stopping a tiny bit short and wondering *Could I have got it if I'd gone a little more?* You don't want to be thinking *Would they have taken less?* Decide on your entry bid and dive in with it. It usually feels good, often exciting. If it doesn't, I would suggest this is not the home for you.

Drip – if there's a counteroffer and you're not at your limit, then make your own counteroffer. Be careful though, slowly increase (drip) the bid by small amounts. Some people will throw loads of extra cash on the table to scare the others off. Sometime even the sales agent will tell you this is a good idea. It's a great idea for the person selling the house as it drives things up quicker and everyone gets a little panicked. Never forget that in this process the agent works for the vendor – not for you, even if they have become your bestie during this process. When a counteroffer comes back, then ask how long you have to consider your position. If they say 24 hours then you should take 23 hours and 59 minutes and put in another offer, a slightly higher one. Who knows, maybe in the meantime the other buyer found something else. A good agent won't sell the house without satisfying themselves that they've squeezed everything they can out of you, so don't panic. If another counteroffer comes back, then repeat the 'drip'. If it doesn't work it will be devastating, but you'll get over it. Life tends to work that way.

I remember early in my career I had cause to use Dad's walk-away tactic and to this day it is something I always recommend people do. I was going for job in a large bank about seven or eight years after my trip to Kusadasi. I was actually quite happy in the role I was in but this bank job was going to offer me experience I wasn't getting in my current role and I really wanted that new challenge. I worked really hard at interview stage to convince the recruiters that not only did they want me but that they needed me. I hope I came across as confident and able without seeming cocky.

The interview process was gruelling enough, particularly as I was only in my early twenties. They really put me through my paces. I remember the third and last interview, in which I had to present a client case study to two senior managers and somebody from HR. They really interrogated me but I felt strong and leaving that one I thought I'd nailed it; in fact the confidence I got from the interview made me want the job even more. My mate Ross was in recruitment in one of the big rival companies at the time. He had helped me prep for the interviews and after this interview I rang him and gave him a debrief. He was confident I had the job in the bag and I was too. He said the only thing still to be decided was which of the two managers would win the battle to get me on their team – because, as he said, 'that's exactly what the fight in the room was after you left'.

This was the early noughties and the salary being advertised was a range of €40–60k basic plus car, pension and other benefits; and if targets were met I had a good chance of earning over €100k. Then the call came from one of the managers, Michael, offering me the job. It all sounded great. I was going to be covering an area that suited me and there were a few other nice things thrown in, such as holidays, that I had not factored in. Then he mentioned the salary: he was offering me €42,000. I was a little taken aback, but asked him his rationale. He explained that I would make good money if I hit targets and reminded me that my current base was €36,000. I understood his rationale and as a poor haggler my temptation was to ask him to let me consider the offer and get off the phone and away from the situation as fast as I could.

Then I thought about what I had learned watching Dad in Kusadasi and decided to deal with it head on. I simply replied, 'Michael, sorry – I've wasted everyone's time, but the package isn't right. Let's just leave it at that.'

Now it was Michael's turn to be surprised. 'What do you mean? It's more than you're currently on. It's more than a 10 per cent pay rise!'

To be fair his maths wasn't wrong, but what he hadn't allowed for was the fact that I was happy in my job, knew I was getting on well and was sure that I could earn the same money overall staying where I was, with less uncertainty around whether I would make it or not. I had gone through this process because a recruitment agent approached me. I was not necessarily looking for a job and I certainly was not unhappy where I was. In that brief moment when Michael mentioned the €42,000 salary I was genuinely of the belief that moving was not worth it for that money and I was happy to walk away.

Michael is a clever guy and my confidence when I apologised for 'wasting everyone's time' obviously made him realise that I wasn't playing games and I was going to walk away. He asked what it would take for me to come across to the team. I said there was no chance I was coming for less than €60,000. He came back two days later with €56,000. I took the job.

I meet Michael from time to time, often in Croke Park. He was a great manager and a really good guy, but he did tell me years later 'You broke my balls' in the negotiation stages of that process. No doubt if he reads this he will dispute how this all went down. But I defo won that one.

I won that one because I watched Dad, not just in Kusadasi but afterwards too. He haggled a lot. Even at home in Ireland, he always asked, 'Is that the best price?' He loved driving from garage to garage looking at new cars or doing his research online when he was buying a new gadget or camera. He got a kick out of it. I don't, but I do appreciate it. I learned from him to do something I don't like and I then found a way to apply it in a way I'm comfortable with. For me, when haggling or bargaining for something, I must first convince myself that I'm genuinely happy to walk away if the deal doesn't go the way I want it to.

Can you teach haggling to kids? Well, with children we should really observe and see how they are with this skill. Then it's about the basics of letting them pay for their sweets in the shop when they are young (no haggling here!), but as they get older it's about them watching you engage with others and more importantly it's about you talking them through your thought process when doing a deal. Let them see your side of it but let them also observe the salesperson's reactions to you. Discussing these things briefly afterwards will have long-term impact on kids. It did on me. Haggling is fun for some – they thrive on it. For others it's a chore. For those of us who don't see it as good craic, it's still important as it stops us getting ripped off. Be mindful of your attitude to it and try to identify what your child's attitude to it is and help them out. This skill for all of us is useful in so many places, whether it's buying a house or a Ralph Lauren shirt on the streets of Kusadasi.

11. Love your savings

In private practice we tend to deal with people who have either established wealth or are HENRYs (high earners not rich yet). In either category, they tend to have learned early on in their lives for one reason or another that having debt, particularly crappy debt like credit card, overdrafts, personal loans and so on is one sure way of not getting rich. The earlier you learn that debt is not your friend, the better.

Each series of *How to Be Good with Money* gets hundreds of applicants who want to come on the show to get on top of their debt. If I do my job right and they do what they're told, by the end of the show they will be on their way to clearing their debt but more importantly they will hate that debt. Later on down their path of financial discovery you'll find that they will start to accumulate some savings. When they do, they begin to love their savings. Saving for them can become addictive. Every time I come across a 20-something with high levels of personal debt, I wish I could have got to them sooner and instilled a love of savings instead of an acceptance that borrowing money is OK.

If as an adult you don't love your savings, it's probably because you haven't been doing it long enough, you've failed to accumulate savings in the past or because you've just never been able to build an amount large enough to make it worth your while investing in it emotionally.

Having savings gives us options. The more you have in savings, the more choices you can make and therefore the more options you have. The earlier we learn the true value of what our savings can buy us the more we can appreciate the importance of building them. But it also means we truly grasp the toxicity of negative savings, i.e. debt.

If savings equals options, and we truly believe that, then it's hard to ignore that debt equals restriction. Saving does appear to come more naturally to some people than to others, but we can absolutely train ourselves to have a savings habit. Loving your savings is the first step, and, let's be fair, that only comes from understanding what those savings can do for you. One thing to watch out for: I have seen people love their savings, spend it all and then never get back on the bandwagon to start saving again because they lose that love. This is never more obvious than when couples save for a house, put it all into the deposit and three years later are still not on the savings bandwagon again. Building savings is hard. Spending it can be easy. But starting again can be even harder than the first time because you know how hard and how long it can take to accumulate decent savings. When you clear yourself of your savings completely, it takes serious willpower to get back saving again, because you know the road ahead.

That's why I recommend that you try never to spend more than half your savings. This way you're not starting from scratch again; you have some momentum and it feels easier. Obviously there will be times when you need to spend more than half, such as the aforementioned example of a house deposit. But when you must break the half rule, try to leave yourself something to springboard off again. You'll be happy you did.

When it comes to encouraging saving habits in children, one of the issues we have in today's financial world – which we all struggle a little with, but it does represent a bigger challenge for children – is the fact that we don't really hold physical cash anymore. We hold most, if not all, of our money electronically in our bank accounts. This causes a significant problem for a child where they can't physically touch the cash, they can't count it out, they can't put it in piles so they can 'budget' what they want to spend it on. Instead, they simply see a number on a screen and it does not hold the same value as a handful of cash would, even if that cash were coins. This is why it's really important to encourage early savings in coins.

As kids get older and inevitably move to electronic banking savings/ transactions, then it's time to implement a different strategy of getting your kids to love their savings. You need to constantly convert the money into things. So if they have €10 in their online wallet then tell them what that could buy, get them to understand its value. Pick stuff up in the shop and say, 'This bar of chocolate, with your savings you could buy ten of these' or 'This ball, you could only buy one of these.'

The more you repeat this exercise, the better. Don't allocate time to sitting down once a week to discuss these things, do it as you go through your week instead. Make it about real life. Try and bring it to things you pay for too, like diesel or a meal out.

You can't do this too much. As the kids get older make it about bigger things, like the mortgage or rent. Most kids love to know how much of Ronaldo's wages they could pay. At the time of writing Ronaldo is earning €25 million a year with Manchester United – if he was working 24 hours a day, seven days a week, 365 days a year then he earns €2,853 per hour (before tax!). Telling a child that their €100 in savings could pay for a little over two minutes of Ronaldo's wages can give them an idea of how much he earns. But it's also useful to flip it around. Again at the time of writing, the average weekly earnings in Ireland is €849.69. That means the child's savings of €100 could pay the average earner to work for almost five hours based on a 40-hour work week.

The lesson for the child, and us adults, is not that a bloke kicking a football makes loads of money – it's about creating a relationship between their money and things it can buy. But it's also about how different things cost different amounts even if those things are just an individual's time.

Making things relative for children is the important thing; helping them to understand that their savings can buy different things and most importantly that it can't buy them everything allows them to want to grow their savings so that they have more options. And attaching real value to money will pay off throughout their lifetime: the lessons a child learns from getting a windfall of cash, for example, around first holy communion or a big birthday, are invaluable. If they blow it all quickly on stuff that doesn't last it's incredibly important that they learn from this. Blowing it is a mistake for several reasons: they have lost an opportunity to truly value having cash, a value that grows the longer you hold on to it; but also they have blown it on stuff that is now useless, broken, eaten, lost or whatever – the fact is that the money is gone. You need to show them a few weeks or months later how they blew it. I don't want you to upset them too much, but they need to face the fact that they had a wad of cash, they blew it and now they have nothing to show for it.

This may sound harsh but I have seen the same things happen to adults – people come into money, like a lotto win or the sale of their business, and they go off on this ridiculous spending spree. They buy stuff they place zero value on, they do have great experiences and go to lovely places but when you sit them down once things have settled down a little bit, the attitude is always very similar. They talk about how they had lost their way, they were spending lavishly on stuff, maybe even nice stuff but actually when they stripped everything back the spending was niggling at them and they were not enjoying themselves any more than they would have had they bought cheaper things or stayed in less expensive hotels. They discover that the things that made them happy before the money are the things that make them happy now. Ideally, they find this out before all the money is gone, but I thoroughly believe they wouldn't have had to blow any money to find it out if somebody had sat them down as a child after they displayed this trait the very first time and helped them to truly understand that blowing your money or your hard-got savings is never a recipe for happiness. Getting them to learn this early is much less expensive than learning it later in life, even if it does feel harsh to rub it in their face that they made a financial mistake. But whether you're teaching the lesson to yourself as an adult, to a friend or to a child, do tread carefully. People can feel stupid after these things, yet it's not about feeling stupid; it's about recognising that things can be done better.

12. Think long term

As adults, we have a problem thinking about our finances in the long term. We struggle to grasp the idea that if we 'eat everything today, we won't have anything to eat later'. Logically, we *know* that one day we will stop working and our salaries will stop, but lots of us still don't make the connection between that and providing for ourselves in the long-term future.

It's incredibly important to introduce children to the necessity of long-term financial thinking as early as possible. As kids, we all remember long school holidays or it taking forever to get to Christmas, yet as we age the weeks, months and years seem to fly by. It's scientifically proven that as we get older time seems to go by faster. As a child we store more mental images in our head about an event, we remember more and file more data about the things we do and we experience. I have seen this with my own kids. They tell me stuff that I don't even remember us doing together. This can be a really valuable tool for you when teaching children about the value of thinking long term, because what will seem like a snippet to you will feel like a long time to them. The importance of children thinking about money and finances long term and developing that ability is that it will help them to think more strategically.

You can go some way towards instilling this value in kids with simple little incentives. For example, if they have some savings burning a hole in their pocket, reward them with an incentive. I did this recently with my teenagers. I give them an allowance. I told them both that they could spend whatever they wanted of their allowance but any money they had left of their allowance in three months' time I would double.

This was an interesting couple of months. Child 1, the one who spends every cent they ever get when it hits their pocket, really found this a difficult task. They wanted to spend but could see how lucrative hanging on to it would be.

Child 2, who had other savings and hence other options, took it in their stride. They were strategic. They simply used their other savings when they needed anything in the three-month period and had the full amount of their allowance at the end of the three months. They both did really well out of this particular little reward scheme, but it was so much easier for child 2 and child 1 felt very hard done by. The time period was long enough to instil the value of long-term thinking relative to their age but it was also short enough to keep them engaged. But it also proved that having savings because you haven't spent some previous income meant child 2 could take full advantage of this lucrative reward scheme.

You might be thinking *But this is of no benefit to me* if you're an adult with no kids and no dad to double your savings. But the reason I designed this incentive for my kids was because it replicates our pension rules. Yes, the maths is different in that I gave them €60 for every €60 they had whereas the government will only give you €40 for every €60 you put into a pension, but the principle was almost identical. You're rewarded for putting money away today for your future and it's much easier to do that if you have a solid foundation of savings to dip into when necessary, to get you through the period while you're maximising the gain you can receive. This is a huge lesson, and even if you don't need or want to enact this kid-friendly replication, it's still something that I hope every reader will take away from this book.

MONEY MYTHS

There are plenty of thoughts, myths, untruths and interesting questions out there about money. Things such as:

▷ The future is crypto

▷ The rich just get richer

▷ Wealth is nature, not nurture

▷ You can always hustle harder

▷ The taxman is the only winner

▷ There's always tomorrow …

The first thing to say is that most of the statements above are useful excuses for our own failure or to help us to understand, in typical Irish begrudging fashion, why somebody else has done so well. Heuristics are the brain's way of working fast, taking shortcuts in order to allow us to process lots of information really quickly and make decisions. These decisions are made based on past experiences, patterns or some other cue we pick up on, quite often intuitively.

Heuristics can be incredibly useful when it comes to making a quick decision about whether you should run from the approaching hungry lion or stay and fight. But the more complex the situation, the more we need to be conscious that patterns, past experiences and other signals can become muddied and that we often suffer with serious confirmation bias, which is where we look for the patterns that will confirm the answer we want to hear. We can also ignore the ones that tell us we are wrong.

That is why it's so important when it comes to money matters that we always question our thoughts and our beliefs, and that we double- and triple-check ourselves on the decisions we have made. I have to do this all the time. I would hate for my advice to fall into the category of 'we do it this way because we have always done it this way'.

In the previous section we looked at good money habits to get into, and this was the first step to getting our financial mindset in the right place. Now we can apply what we've learned to the myths below and challenge these common ways of thinking that may be holding us back.

Myth #1: The future is crypto.

As I mentioned before, cryptocurrencies have been one of the biggest challengers to conventional thinking about wealth creation that the financial world has experienced. There are the lovers and then the naysayers, but interestingly there are few of us who just sit on the fence.

I have found that anytime I have mentioned crypto on social media, the radio or TV that the lovers really, really love it and vehemently defend their chosen crypto currency. It's incredible to watch. If I say anything remotely negative about crypto in the public sphere, I'm immediately targeted and told I haven't got a clue, I'm old school, I'll be left in the dark when it all flushes through. It can get nasty at times but it's the vigour with which people speak up on crypto that is so incredible.

Yet some of their reaction can be explained by heuristics. We know there are people who have made significant amounts of money by buying bitcoin or dogecoin or whatever took their fancy. These people are held up as examples of what can be achieved. There are also people who have a high profile, who make electric cars and fly to space and are leaders in their own field. They are clever and they invested in crypto. So again they are held up as examples of why everyone should be on board with it. Then there are the fund managers – people who manage billions and billions or euro or dollars or whatever – who are also buying up crypto. Again these are held up as an example of why crypto is a sure thing. So if futurists like Elon Musk, fund managers and clever people are putting money into crypto then it must be the right thing to do. But does their money going in mean you should follow them? Before I explain what I think about crypto, let's look at the idea of following the clever money.

We know from 100+ years of stock-market trading that the clever people need the not-so-clever people in order to be able to make money. In stock markets, somebody has to be selling and somebody else has to be buying for a trade to happen. Now, if you're the cleverest person in the room, you need somebody a little less clever than you to take off the stuff you don't want and you also need somebody a little stupid to be willing to sell you something that you see going up in value. I'm being a little simplistic here but the reality is the professionals are selling stuff they no longer place value on and somebody is buying it. Granted the professionals don't have a great track record of getting it right but still, that's how, in simple terms, trades should be working.

When you think about crypto, it will either be mainstream or gone in 10 years from now. If you're already invested in it, then you need to believe it will last the course. But it's also in your interest to convince others it will too. Like I said earlier, if everybody believes in it and has trust in it then it will last. If they don't it won't. So if you try to convince everyone you know to do what you're doing then you've a better chance of your crypto succeeding. Equally if you hear somebody like me saying 'I don't know where it will end up', then you need to knock that down and sometimes these people knock me down with gusto.

I'll say it over and over again, I don't know where crypto will end up. But when I do, I'll let you know. But at that stage it will be too late because it will all either have collapsed or it will be in everyday use everywhere already.

Crypto may be the next big thing but …

Myth #2: 'There is no next big thing, there is only the last big thing.'

It's a statement I have come out with countless times. Technically the statement is not correct, but what I mean is that we don't know what the next big thing is going to be until after the event. From an investing perspective, we can only identify the next big thing by looking at what has happened in the past. This is for several reasons, namely that no investment is a finite journey with a start and a finish.

Let's take Nokia as an example. I heard that kids these days call the 1980s and 1990s 'the late 1900s' so let's go with their terminology! Back in the late 1900s, Nokia could easily have been identified as the next big thing and if you got in any time from around 1995 onwards you certainly felt very clever when the share price was reading at over $62 in the year 2000. If the next big thing was a story with a start and an end and it ended then, well you truly managed to ride the wave of the next big thing. But if you hung on in there, you're still struggling to recoup the losses as 21 years later, the share price is hovering around $5. But incredibly I was able to find an article online asking 'Is Nokia the next big thing?' The article was posted in January 2021.

Take certain investments at a point in time and you can confirm they were the next big thing of that period. But that's with hindsight. The reality is, as Nassim Nicholas Taleb brilliantly outlines in his book *The Black Swan: The Impact of the Highly Improbable*, that in order to back the next big thing you need to back a serious number of losers before arriving at a winner. The cost of the losers will often outweigh the gain of the winner.

Identifying the next big thing would certainly make an interesting roller coaster of research. A quick google throws up everything from whiskey to government bonds, start-ups and tech innovations to NFC and crypto. The list of next big things is endless and, guess what, in years to come one, two, or ten of the thousands of articles will be held up as proof that such and such was a genius in their ability to identify what the next big thing is and here is the article they wrote years ago, which is proof of their Einstein level of superior knowledge of things none of the rest of us understood like they did. These people will then start talking about their new 'next big thing' and the cycle repeats with their commentary fuelling a flurry of followers with cash who think he/she is a genius and predicts all the trends in advance. It can become a self-fulfilling prophecy.

Personally, I prefer to be boring and invest in almost everything. I spread my money across so many sectors, industries, countries and companies that I'm guaranteed to have all the losers, all the winners, all the mediocre companies and I'm also likely to have the next big thing mixed in there somewhere.

Yep, there's a next big thing, but I'll tell what it was after it's already become it.

Myth #3: The rich get richer.

This is a difficult one to dissect. There is no inevitability that if you're rich you're going to become even more wealthy. Lots of rich people have lost their riches. Equally if you're poor (allow me to use the words 'rich' and 'poor' loosely) it's not inevitable that you'll remain poor forever; the world is full of rags-to-riches stories that debunk that idea.

But on balance, I do believe it's harder for the poor to become rich and it's easier for the rich to get richer. Contrary to what many people say, this is not because there is one set of rules for the rich and another set for the poor. The rules are the same for both. In fact, I'm not aware of any rules, tax legislation or laws that are only available to people based on their net worth. However, there is a whole pile of laws and legislation and even financial planning principles that are accessible only to the wealthy because the poor don't have the financial ability to take advantage of them.

My example of the incentive I put in place for my two teenage kids was a perfect example of this – this is the one where I agreed to double whatever they had left of their monthly allowance at the end of the three months. My child who had lots of savings (the 'rich') was able to use their savings to get by in the three months and therefore take full advantage of the incentive. The 'poor' child who had no savings could have bought nothing for themselves for the three months and got the full reward, but the fact is that they're a teenager and there's stuff they just can't resist spending money on.

Trying to have your three months' allowance left at the end of three months so your dad doubles it is not different to what happened during the Special Saving Incentive Accounts module (SSIA). If you're too young to know what the SSIA was, it was a time in Ireland in 2001–2 when we had an issue with inflation. We had handed over the power to control inflation using interest rates to Europe at the beginning of 1999. Therefore the government of the day had to come up with another way to stop us all spending and driving up prices. They came up with the idea that for every €4 you saved they would immediately add €1, turning it into €5. You could actually see the money go into your account each month as you paid it in, although you did have to leave it there for five years. It was a very successful scheme and achieved its goal of getting people to save and lowering inflation. But it but did result in a whole load of new cars being bought when people took their money out five years later!

Even though the rules were the same for everybody regardless of your income level or personal wealth, the SSIA was a great example of the rich getting richer while the poor sat on the sidelines and watched. Firstly, if you were living week to week from pay cheque to pay cheque, you would have had no spare cash to invest in the scheme in the first place. But some less well-off felt it was just too good to miss out on free money and went without in other areas of their lives in order to find the money to save. But then if something happened, they had no other resources available to them and would likely have to cash it in before the five years were up, even if it meant getting hit with penalties.

Meanwhile, if you had some wealth behind you, then you could really take advantage. The maximum you could put into the scheme was £200 punts per month, which later converted to €254. The government then added their €63.50 to it. So you had €317.50 going into your SSIA account each month.

But then there was another step some people were able to take. If you had access to a good financial adviser, then it's likely they would have recommended you invest your SSIA in shares raather than in a bank account, since it was a long-term (five-year) scheme anyway.

I do remember about 18 months or two years into SSIAs being available listening to one of our esteemed politicians on the radio talking about how people who 'gambled' with their SSIA and invested in the stock markets had lost considerably in the first 18 months. He went on to say that essentially they had been greedy and stupid. He also accused financial advisers and anybody connected to the financial world of profiteering and giving bad advice. I'll save myself the solicitor's letter and him the embarrassment and I won't mention the politician's name. But basically he got it so wrong. His attitude was typical of people who look at long-term investments through a pair of short-term glasses.

In simple terms, if you had invested in the European stock market, after 18 months you would have been down about 20 per cent on your money. It didn't feel great. It led to a flurry of people, who were listening to the likes of this politician, running for the hills. Without decent financial planners to stop them making the wrong choice, many moved from shares to a deposit account, thus locking in their loss.

But if they were getting solid advice from a decent financial planner and they left it alone – in other words, they practised my adage of 'invest and forget' – then in the long run they would have come up trumps. Obviously it varied from person to person, depending on the time they started their five-year period (there was a 12-month window in which you could start your SSIA) but I do recall seeing people investing €15,240 of their own money and then getting the €3,800 top-up from the government. Then the underlying fund giving growth on top of it all meant that after tax they came out with €22,000 altogether.

There are figures available that suggest people with a financial planner have 2.5 times the net worth of people who don't when they retire. Is this an example of the rich always getting richer? There are lots of reasons why this could be the case. Firstly, maybe the financial planner is amazing at their job. Secondly, maybe the person had some wealth to start with, which is why they sought out a financial planner in the first place, or lastly, maybe it's a combination of both things. But I do think the SSIA experience shows a real-life situation we can all relate to. People who were advised turned €15,000 into €22,000 after tax over a five-year period because they used a long-term vehicle for a long-term goal instead of using a short-term vehicle (bank/deposit account) for a long-term goal. They didn't do the wrong thing at the wrong time for the wrong reasons, i.e. jump from shares to deposit because shares were doing exactly what we expected them to do, which is go up and down while on their upward trend. Instead, they just stuck with it. They achieved the ideal of invest and forget.

It's likely somebody who didn't have money to fully max out the SSIA would not have had the money to already be engaged with a financial planner. Therefore if they did manage to pull the money together to do it, it was more likely they would have put their money on deposit. To put the shares-based €22,000 after-tax returns into perspective: if you managed to get an interest rate of 1 per cent after tax on a max €254 + €63.50 you might have come out with about €19,500. That's €2,500 less than the person who was rich enough to do it in what I consider to be the right way.

This is an example of the rich getting richer. But it's not always the case. Tony Robbins, in his book *Money: Master the Game*, tells a story of a Mr Theodore Johnson. Mr Johnson earned a 'meagre' $14,000 per year and died in 1991, leaving behind savings of over $70 million. Robbins claims Theodore achieved this by saving $3,000 (or a little over 20 per cent of his wages) every year and then took full advantage of compound interest. It's a great rags-to-riches story but you have to wonder if it's actually true. Could somebody manage to accumulate that much money? Is it really a case of the poor getting rich?

First things first, apparently Theodore retired in 1952. When we consider his salary, using historic inflation figures I can work out that something that cost $14,000 in 1952 cost $384,091 by 2021. Now salaries typically, over long periods of time, go up at a rate greater than inflation. So it's clear that $14,000 in 1952 was hardly the salary of a 'poor' person. Theodore was on decent wedge.

Putting aside Theodore's decent wages, it was still interesting to suggest he could have amassed over $70 million by the time he died in 1991. If he invested a flat $3,000 per annum into the stock markets between the years 1922 and 1952, he could have contributed $90,000. Overall between 1922 and 1952, the S&P 500 (a stock market that invests in the largest 500 companies based on their financial size/market cap in the US and an accepted US stock-market benchmark) returned over 10 per cent per annum. For the maths to work, Theodore needed just under 13.5 per cent per annum to make the first part of the equation work. The first part was to accumulate enough cash by the time he reached retirement for the second half of the equation to work. The second half is about the money he had at retirement, growing without new contributions and going into a total in excess of $70 million by the time he died 39 years post-retirement in 1991.

For Theodore to have $70 million by the time he died in 1991, he needed to have $968,000 when he retired in 1952. That's because between 1952 and 1991 the S&P 500 grew by 11.6 per cent per annum. He would need $968,000 on the day he retired for it to grow by 11.6 per cent per annum to reach $70 million by the time he died. So the flaws in Robbins's story are potentially that he took somebody who was in fact on a very decent salary and portrayed them as a rags-to-riches story. This person would also have had to achieve 13.5 per cent growth per annum during his working life to amass a lump of $968,000 by the time he retired and then finally that he was able to leave his riches untouched until he died in 1991.

But I do believe the story overall is plausible; just maybe some of the finer details have been airbrushed a little. It's a great story though, and if you listen to how Tony Robbins communicates it then it really hits home. If you do something simple, something small and repeat it over and over again it can have huge results. The little things done right and repetitively are the most impactful of all.

When you think about those rich people who became poor, often times they don't get so poor that they can't have turkey for Christmas but they have lost significant amounts of money. But it interests me when you delve a little deeper on these things: wipe-out stories tend to have one similar theme in common when you look under the surface and that is that the people who lost the money all seemed to lack diversification. In other words, they had all their eggs in one basket.

I have heard countless stories from clients where they had amassed serious wealth for themselves. This may have been through regular savings, inheriting money, selling their business or winning the lotto. They were then at a crossroads waiting to make their next move. Imagine it is circa 2007 and their friendly bank manager told them, 'Interest rates in bank accounts are very poor right now. I know you're waiting to make your next business move with this money but in the meantime why don't you buy some shares in the bank rather than letting it waste away in the deposit account?' Seemed like a plausible option and sure the bank manager said they always paid a decent dividend and the bank manager himself has a big chunk of them. Then the bottom falls out the financial world and these bank shares fall apart.

Or else you have the story of the person who builds a property empire, doesn't know when to stop because they have never worked out how much is enough and they do one BIG deal. It puts everything at risk but if they pull it off, it will be time to retire to a beach somewhere. They know deep down it won't be the last one but they love the buzz of it all. Then something goes wrong, the banks circle the wagons, force the sale through at the most inopportune time and the person is left with nothing while the banks are fully covered.

What fascinates me about people who are rich is that when they get knocked down they tend to get back up again. I have a theory that's not based on any fact, but in typical confirmation-bias fashion the world keeps sending me signs that say, 'Yes Eoin, you're right, your theory is bang on.' My theory is that we are heavily influenced by the people we are surrounded by. Surround yourself by people with a crap negative attitude and you will become negative. Surround yourself by driven, successful people and you'll become successful and driven. Surround yourself by rich people and you'll become rich.

I'm not saying that you'll become rich by osmosis. But I do believe that if you see being rich as the 'norm', things become very relative. If all your friends are heading for nice meals, trips away and enjoying life, it's possible you'll work to try to find a way to have the financial ability to keep up with them. If the opposite is the case, that you surround yourself with people who spend very little because they don't have it, then you may not see it as 'normal' to have money and therefore you may find it more difficult to believe you should.

Please don't take me up wrong, I totally accept it's not black and white. But if we believe in something, we can often achieve it. So I'm simply taking my theory one step further and saying that if wealth is in your face all day every day it takes less imagination to attract yourself to nice things. This is not about keeping up with the Joneses; I'm simply talking about the idea that if your friend comes home from an amazing trip, sits you down and tells you all about it, then it's easier for you to imagine you doing that too. But if you're broke and your friends and family are broke it's much harder to ever imagine that you'll shortly be heading to a five-star resort in the Maldives. But I'm strong believer that you could. It's possible for the rich to get richer, the poor to stay poor but also for either group to jump to the other cohort from doing the right or the wrong things.

I'll acknowledge one thing, however, and that is that some people struggle badly with money: they have so little coming into their household that breaking the cycle may feel impossible. What I would say to these people is that the tiniest of changes can have a dramatic impact. For example, I remember the single mother who told me that because of my advice she had savings for the very first time in her adult life (of course it was her actions not my advice that meant she now had savings). If my memory serves me correctly she had been saving €5 per week and had accumulated a pot of €60. I genuinely believe this saving was worth more to her than a rich client who had €600,000 in savings. But more importantly the changes she had made to her spending did not have a negative impact on her life that was greater than the positive impact the savings were having. She had also created a habit and, most importantly, she had real financial pride in what she had achieved. For the first time in her adult life she was getting ahead financially. That €60 was worth its weight in gold. She, in her own way, was bucking the 'poor stay poor' story.

But let's be up front here: rich people do have it easier. When I look at clients who have attended private secondary schools I'm often intrigued about their opinion of it now as adults. They often talk about how the facilities were great; the teachers were very good but they also argue that ultimately your results came down to yourself; they do not believe they would have got any better or any worse results had they been to a non-fee paying school. They are quite convinced of this.

But when you delve into it, you really get to understand the hidden advantages of private education. It's in their network. Their mates are now in positions where they are head of x, or among the top barristers in the country, or brilliant surgeons. Why? Probably because their mother or fathers did the same thing before them. They saw that their parents were surgeons so they believed they could be surgeons. It was plausible. It was identifiable and, therefore, could be achieved.

But this network can also allow these people who had a good financial start to have access to great minds. They have access to people excelling in their career. They have access to people who are earning good money. These people are their friends and if you're trying to raise money for your new business venture it can be very useful to have friends with money. Even if things fall apart for you, there's often a mate who can help pick you up. Or the top accountant mate who makes sure the financial impact of the fall isn't as long term as it might have been.

Surrounding yourself with people who are brilliant at what they do allows you also to become brilliant at what you do. It gives you somebody to bounce ideas off. It's having a strong network of people to call on for advice.

I do think the rich have it easier, but I don't believe the system is designed to help them. The very wealthy do worry about the poor catching up. The next time you hear somebody very rich arguing for higher taxes, listen carefully to the type of taxes they want to see getting raised. Oftentimes you'll hear them argue that capital taxes, such as how much tax you pay when you sell a property or a business, should be low to encourage people to invest in future developments and business and thus advance the world. But they are often in favour of higher income taxes. In very simple terms, this is because they are sitting on huge amounts of capital. The more the people coming up the wealth ladder behind them get taxed on their income, the less income they will have to invest and catch the rich people. We can see this in our tax system: we have high capital gains taxes but even higher income taxes. Does this say the system favours the rich? Perhaps. But is it because of some conspiracy theory that the rich help the rich get richer? I think that's a bit of a leap.

If the rich are clever, they do get richer. But I don't believe that is necessarily to the detriment of the poor. The options afforded to rich are also available to the poor, it's just poor may not be able to take advantage of them – yet.

When it comes to rich getting richer, I do recall a common trait in a lot of people who were doing exceptionally well out of property deals prior to the global financial crisis of 2008. They were all kind of acting blindly. It may sound harsh, but I suspect some of them lacked the patience – or possibly the intelligence – to fully think things through. They made exceptionally risky deals, fuelled by banks giving out loans at ridiculous levels to anybody who was willing to take them. Due to these investors' rashness, they didn't have the same fear that an analytical, critically thinking person would have had; they just leapt in and made serious money on a market that was going up and up and up. They then used their success to fuel more deals. With this in mind, I would maintain that if you're clever and rich it's very easy to do well. If you're clever and poor, it may be more difficult, but you can still do well. It's less likely, if you're not-so-clever and poor, that you'll get out of that trap. But if you're not-so-clever and *rich*, you can also do very well. For a period. Then at some point you'll either do the deal that breaks you or the market, or your investing/gambling will collapse around you.

The property rush that went on prior to 2008 displays stark similarities to something we may be witnessing today. A cohort of people taking risks, riding a wave, believing that it's not the market movements but their own genius that is making them richer, sneering at anybody who is not involved and attacking those who would question the validity of what they are doing and what they are investing in. I am, of course, talking about crypto investors/gamblers. They do have the advantage over property investors in that they're not borrowing to invest in crypto, but otherwise the similarities are incredible when you compare them with 2007 property investors. I hope that the outcome for those with money in crypto doesn't end in the type of financial ruin that some people who bet on property were left with.

Myth #4: I don't earn enough money to think about my financial future.

Very few people have the ability to control how much they earn. Many self-employed people have limited ability to generate more income or take more from their businesses. There are people who are in a job they love and don't want to move even for more money. Then there are people who don't have either the skills or the confidence to go after that promotion or apply for a better-paid job. So I accept that a lot of people, due to their circumstances, have no control over how much they earn. But everybody has control over what they *spend*.

Theodore Johnson in the Robbins story controlled his spending and saved a little over 20 per cent of what he earned. I know inflation figures and the time value of money kind of diluted the impact of this story but we can't take away from the simple maths. Even the single mother, who was on minimum wage and was fully accustomed to spending every single penny that came in every single week, still found €5 a week and saved it consistently for 12 weeks. Life on minimum wage is incredibly tough. I accept that completely and I thank my lucky stars each and every day that I do not have to do it. But if that woman can find €5 a week I do believe you could find €1 or €0.50 or even less each week that you could put away.

I was involved in *This Crowded House*, a TV show presented by Brendan Courtney. The concept of the show was that Brendan went into a house that had an adult child living in it. They either had never moved out or they had moved out but for whatever reason had to move home again (boomerang kids). Brendan effectively became their mate for the duration of the show and as part of their process of moving out to rent or to buy he brought them to see me to get them financially fit for their move.

There was one particular person on the show who I'll always remember. He was father to a young boy and was paying maintenance to his child's mother. He was living at home with his mother and his sister. He earned about €320 per week after tax and was not enjoying his job. He really wanted to become a mechanic and during the course of the show he was offered an apprenticeship. The problem was his take-home pay was going to drop to €230 per week if he followed his heart and started to train to be a mechanic. He felt he couldn't afford to do it and continue to maintain his life and support his child. He would be down €90 per week. He was stuck.

Now this was an easy one for me as the financial planner. I took one look at his finances and explained to him that over the last five years I estimated he had spent €26,000 on cigarettes. He was spending €100 per week on cigarettes when I met him. If he gave up and took the drop in salary to become a mechanic he would be up €10 per week. I have given up cigarettes, I know how hard it is. But this was not just about giving up for the sake of his health. This was his career, his son, his lifestyle and his pocket.

It would be nice if you could look at your finances and see the wasted €100 a week you have been spending all this time stare back at you in the face. Not all of us will have such a eureka moment. But there are the lesser things. The average saving for moving your gas and electricity provider is about €25 per month. Do you use all your Netflix, Amazon Prime, Apple TV and Sky subscriptions? How about Spotify and Apple Music? If we look hard enough, we can find things in our lives that are either excessive or, more importantly, don't add value to our lives. Particularly by identifying stuff that doesn't add value – things we just have because we always have – and getting rid of them, you can save money without any reduction in the quality of your life. That's what true budgeting, or as I like to call them 'spending rules', is for. It's about spending less money on the things that add no value to your life so that you have more money to spend on the things that do.

You might think that the small stuff has little or no impact. But you're wrong on two counts. Firstly, the little things done frequently and repetitively will create huge results over time. Secondly, this is where a lot of us often fall down. Frequent questions on my Instagram Q&A might be along the lines of, 'I only have €500 to put away for five+ years – is there any point?' Let's face it. The rules, reason, method and rationale for investing €5 million are exactly the same as the rules, reason, method and rationale for investing €500. Of course it makes sense. Moreover, the charges on pensions and investments are usually percentage based so they are actually, by default, designed to work for big or small sums. The excuse that you don't earn enough is, in my opinion, a get-out-of-jail card. Money is relative. If you can even afford to save 1 per cent of your wages, after doing that 100 times you'll have an entire wage packet saved. The numbers don't actually matter, it's down to percentages.

There may be one thing I'm overlooking and that is we all require a basic living wage. This is the amount of money we need to clothe and feed ourselves and to put a roof over our heads. Once we reach this, then in theory we should be able to save the rest. In practice, however, life kicks in. I find it really interesting when I work with a family for a period and then someone loses their job. Each year as their salaries rose, so too did the cost of running their lives. Each pay rise brought with it more spending. Then all of sudden that income disappears. This is an awful shock – emotionally, mentally and financially.

But I witness something immediately that the people going through it often identify on reflection, after the event, when everybody in the house is back in work. What happens when there's a loss of salary is that lifestyle immediately adjusts. It's 'lifestyle creep' – when your spending inches upwards in line with your salary – in a dramatic reversal. All of a sudden the absolute 'must-haves' go. The family feel no shame in cutting things. They do it because they have to. But people who go through this enforced adjustment very often don't allow lifestyle creep to begin again once the money starts flowing. People who experience the loss of one income adjust for the loss and then realise there is a whole pile of stuff they don't actually miss. This results in them never quite going back to their old way of spending.

Thankfully you don't have to go through a global pandemic or lose your job to reverse the lifestyle creep. It's about sitting by yourself if it's just you, or sitting with your partner and maybe even your kids if it's appropriate, and identifying what stuff you would cut if you were forced to. What would be the first, second and third thing to come off the list? This is actually a tough question to answer because we can be soft on ourselves.

'I could give up the second mini-break I'm taking next year, but why should I? I work hard. I don't get quality time with my partner. I deserve it.'

Guess what? I don't disagree with you. You do deserve it but if you want your financial future to change, you might have to change what you're doing today in order to achieve that. If you have good money coming into the house, the decisions of what you're cutting may feel really hard. But it's much easier to make those decisions now, out of choice, than at some stage in the future when you've lost your job and these decisions are forced on you because you don't have the financial structure in place to ride the wave.

If you don't have a strong salary coming into the house this is an even tougher review to do. You're looking at cutting what others might consider basics. You might be talking about buying own-brand ice cream instead of the really expensive stuff – or even no ice cream – just so you can save €1, €2 or €3 this week. The sacrifices are different but the outcomes are relative and therefore also beneficial. Maths is not discriminatory: the benefits of investing loads of money apply also to the benefits of investing small amounts of money.

I remember I was at my friend Collie's stag party. We were at the Galway Races. One of his mates, who I knew of but didn't know well, and I were looking over the race programme, picking out the horses we were going to back. I hadn't a scooby doo what I was looking at. He did. As the day went on he laughed at me arriving back from the tote.

'How did you get on?' he asked.

I explained I had won, but what he found hilarious was that I had put down €5, won and got my €5 plus €3. I got a total of €8. He just couldn't understand what the point was with either betting that amount or at those odds. I was genuinely perplexed. You see, if I sat with a client and said, 'Give me €5 million and in 20 minutes I'll give you back your €5 million plus another €3 million,' then all my clients would be signing up each and every time. So why then doesn't it make sense to turn €5 into €8?

Thankfully, the rules of financial planning are not based on how much you're worth. Neither are the rules of investing. Everyone should be investing in their financial future regardless of their salary. Just do the little things frequently enough and you'll get big results. But more importantly, we all need to control our controllables. Most people can't control what they earn most of the time, but we can all control what we spend. Concentrate on the stuff you can do and don't waste energy on the stuff you can't do.

Myth #5: Wealth is nature, not nurture.

People can be born with a silver spoon in their mouth. It helps, it's a stepping stone into creating more wealth. Because as we identified earlier, if you're born into a family of privately educated, land-owning wealthy people, then it's likely your mother is best friends with the top barristers in the country and your dad was best man for one of the top CEOs in Europe. In other words, they have connections and you have a pre-loaded network to tap into. Good old nepotism is alive and well.

But that doesn't mean you can't mess it up, or at the very least it doesn't mean you can always make the most of it. I have clients who, from the outside, have all the trappings of wealth but can't afford to heat the manor house they live in. If you create your own wealth and lose it, then it can be very difficult to face the world. But if you're handed wealth and lose it then there is a different level of family guilt and shame levelled on you. Sometimes if you're lucky enough to be born into money you can do okay with it; make yourself look like a business genius because you're wealthy to begin with, but when you do a bit of research you find there's actually no genius involved here. You started rich and got a little richer, but actually you could be a lot further on based on where you started from.

When I think of this, Donald Trump always comes to mind. He was born into a family with a lot of property or, as they say over there, real estate. His parents gave him a ton of money to start him off. He disputes the amount he was given, of course he does. But let's look at the maths: he is extremely wealthy today, but is he the business genius he claims to be or did he actually not do so well over the years?

Let's load the answer with the fact that he has filed for bankruptcy several times (we won't hold that against him – falling into bankruptcy in the States is a badge of honour, often for tax purposes, and is almost an accepted part of the job for some people creating real wealth in the US). But what do we actually know about his wealth? As you might imagine, every time the likes of *Forbes* magazine announces what his wealth is he disputes it and claims it to be considerably higher than reported.

Firstly, Trump, who claims to be a self-made millionaire, even disputes how much he was given by his father to start him off. He says he was given a loan of $1 million, yet there is strong suggestion it was actually in excess of $60 million and there are reports most of it was never paid back – more like a silver shovel than a silver spoon. Regardless of how he got started, if we look at where he was in the early eighties and compare it to today, we can get some idea of how he has done.

In 1982 Trump, as usual, disputed the figure published in *Forbes*: it said he was worth $200 million; he said he was worth $500 million. In 2020 *Forbes* claimed his net worth was $2.5 billion. He has been less vocal since he left the White House about disputing his net worth so let's just use this figure of $2.5 billion as his current wealth.

If you use his $500 million starting point back in 1982 and if he had sat on a beach for the past 38 years instead of going to the hassle of building his property empire, could he have done better? Let's say he had put the money in the S&P 500 instead, (the stock market index of the largest 500 companies in the US). The S&P has grown by over 12 per cent per annum for the 38-year period. Trump turned €500 million into $2.5 billion in that period based on his own numbers, at a growth rate of just over 4.3 per cent per annum. Even using the $200 million reported by Forbes in 1982 instead of his figures it is a growth rate just under 6.9 per cent per annum.

But – and here's the kicker – if he had sat on a beach and invested his $200 million back in 1982, he would have made over 12 per cent per annum. Instead of being worth $2.5 billion 38 years later he would have been worth over $16 billion using a starting point of $200 million, or he would be worth more than $41 billion if his starting figure of $500 million is correct.

In other words it has cost Trump at least $13.5 billion because he tried to do it himself. He should have sat on that beach.

We don't have to look as far as the *Forbes* richest list to find examples of people who are born into wealth then mess things up. In Ireland, 75 per cent of all companies are family-run. I'm not suggesting everyone who owns a family business is loaded but the sector does provide for interesting data in terms of passing wealth from one generation to another. Of these family businesses, only 30 per cent successfully pass down to the second generation and only 10 per cent make it to the third generation. This is stark and does suggest that if the wealth is tied up in the business, there is a 70 per cent chance that the business won't be in the family for long.

The reasons given for this apply to the passing on of any type of wealth to another generation. If an offspring comes into a family business, in some cases they get the job because of who they know as opposed to what they know. It's not their ability that gets them the job, it's their lineage. This can result in them being a little more laid-back about their responsibilities and can in turn lead to poor results for the company. Obviously I'm not saying this is the case for every person who ever ends up working with their mother or father, but the stats of a 70 per cent failure rate do suggest there are some issues in passing on a business.

These traits can also be attributed to the passing on of wealth. Films in particular have often portrayed the spoilt rich kid who has little or no respect for money, has zero drive and probably has some type of substance-abuse issue. Again I'm not say everybody born into wealth has a problem with drugs but I can think of at least a half dozen people I have come across in my life who because they were born into wealth have a lack of respect for money and a serious sense of entitlement. The sense of entitlement results in them feeling they are deserving of everything without the need to try, have it hard or in fact go through any level of pain in order to get what they want. These people sit back and expect the world to serve them up their dreams and when it doesn't they can behave like spoilt children who didn't get what they demanded from Santa.

There is, of course, the opposite: the people born into wealth who want to make their own way in life. They have the contacts and all the support of the money in the family. They also have a confidence instilled in them by watching people around them succeed at what they do. These people want to do things for themselves and they want to find their own way and can become incredibly successful.

To sit back and think to yourself *I wasn't born into money so there's no point in trying* would be a ludicrous direction to take. You may not have the same springboard as somebody who was born into wealth. You may also have some of the odds stacked against you, but it's still very much within your grasp to achieve financially and control your own financial destiny, to educate yourself financially and to work towards the things you want. I have watched very successful people who have come from a weaker financial background: these people not only appreciate it more but they also learned more along the way and are therefore less likely to lose it all.

It's also likely that they will have a better ability to pass the wealth on. Lots of my clients who build their own wealth have a strong attitude that they want their kids to be supported but also want to make sure that they learn to paddle their own canoe. They recognise that there were valuable lessons learned in the process of creating their wealth and they don't want their kids to miss out on those lessons.

One particular business-owner springs to mind. They set up a company well over 50 years ago and now have their children working in the family firm. But they had some rules before they came into the company. The first was they had to work somewhere else for a minimum of five years after college before they could come into the family business. They were then hired by management for a role that they were qualified to do and were interviewed in the same way everybody else was. This person wasn't running a family business, they were running a business that happened to have family in it. Not all the children decided to join the business. Of the ones that did, not all went into management and at the time of writing I know of at least one of the sons who has been front line in the business since they joined more than five years ago. They feel no sense of entitlement and know they will progress based on their merit. Interestingly, when you talk to them about it they would not have it any other way.

Deciding whether or not a person's financial destiny is based on what wealth they are born into has too many variables to provide a conclusive answer. There are rich kids who will end up poor and poor kids who will end up rich. Do I believe that we all have our financial future written in our DNA from birth? This is actually semi-plausible. Some of us are born greedy, selfish, generous or kind – or are we? Do we learn these traits in early life? I don't know. But what I do know is that whatever way you enter life, whatever financial habits you learn in life, good or bad, they can all be changed. I have seen people who could never save become savers. I have seen people who hate spending money and would be considered tight become spenders.

The spenders are always interesting to me. Going through a financial planning process, I can calculate, based on a person's current wealth and expected expenditure, how much more that person can spend each year so as not to worry about money. This is where our understanding of the financial personality type becomes really important, particularly in a couple. We will often identify early on that one is a spender and one is a saver. One worries about the future and the other thinks, *Sure we could all be gone tomorrow, let's enjoy today*. A good financial plan will satisfy both: address the financial future and allocate money from today to cover it, meaning that anything left over is guilt-free spending.

A good financial planner, however, is also trying to make sure each person in the financial plan is happy. We must read the room – most of the time the person driving the engagement with us in the first place is the one who worries about the future, but we also have an obligation to the other person who wants to enjoy today. We need them to buy into the plan too or it will never work. That's why we can often work out how much over and above their current expenditure somebody can spend without blowing up their long-term financial future. But telling somebody who is living for today you can spend €X amount more per year can be a dangerous thing to do, because often €X becomes a target not a limit.

A financial plan is often a turning point in people's financial personalities. If they have always been frugal but are confident in the plan, they will suddenly be more willing to spend. This can be a brilliant moment for a couple who have been playing financial tug-of-war with each other for years: all of sudden they are spending on guilt-free weekends away, safe in the knowledge they can actually afford it. But if the plan dictates that some tightening of expenditure is required, then the person who 'lives for today' is more likely to row in behind if they can see a trade-off: for example, if I don't do the extension on the house it means I can stop working two years earlier. Financial planning is about turning the numbers into real life so we can see what our money helps us to achieve.

Having watched hundreds if not thousands of people go through the process and change behaviours and habits of a lifetime, I believe that, regardless of ingrained wealth, money creation and financial habits are controllables and can be changed.

Myth #6: We should all aim for FIRE.

Of all the financial movements, goals, strategies and hare-brained ideas, this is the one I want to see succeed more than anything, but I do fear for its foundations. Some of the maths is questionable.

FIRE stands for Financial Independence Retire Early. The concept behind it is that people save a very large portion of their income in their twenties and thirties to be able to stop working altogether and retire in their thirties or forties. They restrict themselves in order to achieve their goal of being financially independent at a very early stage in life.

There are two types of FIRE: fat or lean. Fat FIRE is where you create enough wealth to earn yourself a nice lifestyle when you stop working. Lean FIRE is about continuing with the restricted life you have lived in order to achieve FIRE in the first place. It would not be unusual for people to be saving 50–75 per cent of their wages each month. The end goal is to build a pot that will generate the income they need to live their lives and to achieve this as early as possible.

If you start very early on in your career, then saving 50–75 per cent of your wages is actually quite achievable. When I'm invited to speak to graduating college students I often discuss the concept of Parkinson's law. This states that the length of time you have to do a job determines how long it will take you to complete the job. For example, if you have an hour to cut the grass then it will take an hour to cut the grass, but if you have three hours it will take three.

The same thing applies to your income. I have clients who live very happy and comfortable lives earning a combined salary of, let's say, €100,000 per annum and then I have clients who also live happy and comfortable lives earning €1 million per annum. One is not necessarily ten times happier than the other because of the difference in their salaries. But, more importantly, when you ask them both if they enjoyed the salary increases they got over the years they will often look confused. In fact, ask yourself when you got your last pay rise and how much you enjoyed it. Most people will say 'What pay rise?' As our wages go up, so too does our lifestyle, which expands to fill the income we have. It's Parkinson's law.

When I speak to graduates I try as best I can to convey the enormity of their first pay cheque. Most are going from part-time work or no work to getting a monthly income for the very first time – likely the biggest 'pay rise' they ever get. Lifestyle creep has yet to kick in; they have always managed to live on very little up to now so they have a choice. They can either become accustomed to their new income or they can make life-lasting decisions now. If they have heard about the FIRE movement and if they are motivated enough by its potential outcome then this is the best time in their career to actually chase that dream. They have been living off close to zero up to that point so living off 25 per cent and saving 75 per cent is feasible before life kicks in.

Getting your first 'real' job is a great time to aggressively start saving and it means it feels like less of a sacrifice because instead of cutting out or giving up stuff from your life you're just not letting things *into* your life. But if you're not fortunate enough to currently be in your early twenties, don't despair – all is not lost for you to take full advantage of preventing the effects of Parkinson's law.

There was an interesting piece of research I studied during my postgrad that looked at people's willingness to save some of their salary for a pension. People can be quite reluctant or even a little worried about putting some of their current salary away for their long-term financial future. They worry about signing forms that commit them to this. This is evident in the whole area of 'auto-enrolment'.

The current concept in Ireland is that if you join a company and they have a pension scheme for which you're eligible you need to fill out the forms and you join the scheme. Auto-enrolment reverses this. What happens is that when you join a company with a pension scheme you have to fill out forms if you *don't* want to join the pension scheme. You automatically join the scheme if you don't do any paperwork. Countries that have auto-enrolment in place have seen the participation in pensions across the board go from under 50 per cent to close to 90 per cent. We are due to introduce this is in Ireland in the coming years – it was supposed to be 2022/23 but certain deadlines have not been met, so it's unlikely to happen any time soon. Auto-enrolment gets over certain behavioural blocks for people joining pensions, such as 'I don't know how to join' and 'I don't know what fund to pick' – because they don't have to do anything and there will be a default fund. 'I'll do it later' is overcome by the fact that there is hassle filling out the forms. 'I don't know how much to put in' – there are standard defaults for contribution levels. But, most importantly, auto-enrolment overcomes the concern people have about proactively making a decision to sacrifice salary today for the benefit of the future. When it's automatic, it feels like a decision is being made for you and therefore you're less likely to catastrophise that decision, worrying all about the what-ifs.

I see this a lot with people who hit tough times and cancel their pension contributions until 'things get better'. When people are doing this, we always encourage them to put a definitive timeframe on it. If you have hit rough times to the point that you have to stop payments going into your pension, no bell is going to ring one day that lets you know, *Guess what, the tough times are over.* So when you stop the payments we always encourage people to suspend payments for three or six months instead. That way they start up again automatically in six months without you having to decide to start them. If things are still bad when they are due to start up again, you just postpone by another three to six months at that point. You can use the same behavioural trait to reverse the idea of lifestyle creep. When people were asked to invest some money today into their pension, they were slow to take it up. But when people were asked today to sign a form to commit a portion of their future pay rises to their pension, a far higher percentage of people agreed.

We are, generally, positive about our financial future. Yet we are uncomfortable committing income we are already accustomed to but are happy to commit income we have yet to get. If you're not just out of college, this is the way you can slow down the progressions of lifestyle creep. But if you're 42 years old, future pay rises may not cut it to allow you to achieve FIRE any time soon: you'll need to make dramatic changes to achieve it so it's about deciding if it *is* worth it.

One concern I have for the FIRE movement is that their maths is based on research carried out in 1994 by William Bengen, who developed the 4 per cent rule: according to Bengen, if you draw 4 per cent out of an investment pot each year then you should in most circumstances survive your retirement without running out of money. In simple terms, if you need €40,000 per annum then you need a pot of €1 million to sustain this income for your retirement. So people trying to achieve FIRE have their goal, work out how much they need to live off, divide it by four and multiply it by 100 to work out how much of a pot to accumulate.

If you're reaching for the calculator on your phone just now, let me make it easier on you – see the table below:

The Bengen Rule	
Desired income	Lump sum required under Bengen
€1,000	€25,000
€5,000	€125,000
€10,000	€250,000
€20,000	€500,000
€30,000	€750,000
€50,000	€1,250,000
€75,000	€1,875,000
€100,000	€2,500,000

Using the €1,250,000 target: if you were on a €50,000 salary and had a 20-year timeframe in mind to reach FIRE, you would need 6 per cent growth and you would need to save €2,705 per month for 20 years to achieve the target of €1,250,000. Earning €50,000 you should have take-home pay of €3,067 per month after tax. So you would need to save 88 per cent of your salary and I've taken some short cuts: I've ignored taxes on the investment and I've assumed a 6 per cent growth on the investment. Living your life on 12 per cent of your salary for 20 years is just the start of my concerns for the entire FIRE movement. I know my calculations are quick but it's the assumptions for growth that really have me concerned for a 40-year-old thinking of packing in their job.

Bengen did his research in 1994 and he used historical data. I accept that it's less than 30 years ago but the data today is already quite different. We are in an unprecedented low-interest-rate environment. There is a direct relationship between low interest rates and lower expected returns from things like shares. In its simplest form, if interest rates are high, then in order to be attractive, shares need to be 'promising' higher returns and when interest rates are low, then the riskier stuff does not have as much pressure on it. Very long-term returns for shares have been circa 8–10 per cent per annum. When I build a financial plan for a private client, I want it to work on an expected return of 4.5 per cent, which is my estimate of what returns their investment will get in their long-term financial future. I know my estimate will be wrong, but I'm also quite confident that it will be on the right – that is, the lower – side of wrong. If I estimate 4.5 per cent and get 6 per cent, then the client is a little better off than I had planned for, they won't be disappointed and their financial plan will work. But if I estimate 8 per cent and get 6 per cent, then their financial plan blows up.

This is my first issue with some of the FIRE calculations: Bengen's rule says the safe withdrawal rate is 4 per cent per annum, but that 4 per cent was calculated at a very different time from a very different starting point. My second issue is in the fact that Bengen's 4 per cent withdrawal rate was based on a 30-year-retirement time horizon. In other words, he was probably thinking of a 60-year-old retiring and living until 90. But if you're retiring at 40 you have 50 years until you get to 90 (to me even 90 is too young to plan towards nowadays; at our practice we plan towards age 100 for every client). Bengen's rule suggest that there is an 80 per cent chance based on his historical data that if you withdraw 4 per cent per year from your retirement pot you won't have run out of money within 30 years. However, if you look at a 50-year time horizon, the probability of not running out of money drops to 30 per cent.

My last issue is that the numbers are different when we move away from the US stock and look at historical data for the UK and Europe. There is a guy in the UK that I have huge amounts of time for, called Abraham Okusanya, who has developed an app that financial planners use called Timeline (timelineapp. co). I recall him presenting at a conference I attended a few years back when he showed data suggesting that the current, safe withdrawal rate in the UK was closer to 3.2 per cent.

So FIRE is concerning for me on a couple of fronts; I really would like to see people achieving it, but I worry about the maths and expectations for growth on which they are basing their entire financial future. It doesn't seem clear to me that the calculations have kept track with modern-day life. I know there is a lot more to the FIRE movement, and honestly I'm a big fan of anybody who can achieve it, but I just hope they tread cautiously and carefully. It will be hard at 62 to try and convince a potential employer that you gave up work at 36 with all the right intentions.

Myth #7: You can always hustle harder.

Whenever you consider the American dream, it always revolves around the idea that hard work will be rewarded. It's the capitalist way. My mother has her own version of this. She always told us, 'Just get the piece of paper'; her way of emphasising the importance of our education. She always felt that if we could get a good solid education, it would set us up for life.

I do believe a strong work ethic is really important. I do believe that, to achieve everything you want to achieve, you need to work hard. For most people, things won't be handed to them on a plate if they put no work in, and nobody can argue with that. But I also believe that there's a limit to this. There comes a point where you can't physically or mentally work any harder and if you do, the level of productivity or the quality of your work deteriorates. I take this approach in my private practice. We believe that if you work late on a Tuesday then you're less useful come Thursday afternoon. In fact, we believe that to some extent fewer working hours can result in more productivity. That's why this summer we trialled a four-day working week.

Previously, we always took a half-day on Fridays in July and August. This year we decided to challenge that a little further: if you could get all your work done from Monday to Thursday then there was no expectation for you to work on Fridays. The company was still expected to provide the same level of service to our clients; we just wanted to see whether, by focusing, we could deliver this in a shorter working week. As I write, we are currently reviewing our findings and talking to staff and clients, but so far it has been received very positively.

This experiment underlines that hard work is important – but working hard and working smart are two different things. Sometimes I feel that 'working smart' sounds like code for 'lazy work', but it really isn't. To me, the only way you can truly be productive while working extremely long hours is to work at something you love. This is where the side hustle comes in.

A side hustle only works long term if it's a hobby you've somehow monetised, or if it's something you get a kick out of doing. The side hustle needs to feel like your hobby and not like your job. This needs to be the case so that it's a break from work as opposed to just more work. You're not working longer hours – it's recreation that you're being paid for. A side hustle that feels like a hobby and pays you money is something that often develops into a full-time job, resulting in you ditching your old job once you feel you can really give it a go. It's the manifestation of the saying, 'Work at something you love and you'll never work a day in your life.'

But if your side hustle doesn't bring you any joy, then it's just another job. I don't believe it's sustainable long term; it's more likely taking away from your ability to do your 'real' job, and the energy you're expending on it would be better spent on achieving better results in your full-time job. We have a finite number of different buckets of hours in our week. We have good productive time, we have good recreation time, we have good relaxation time and so on. The ideal is that you find a job that feels like fun to do – and helps you to relax.

There's been a surge in reported symptoms of burnout in recent years, especially since the pandemic-related rise of home-working, so it's impossible to suggest that hustling with no end in sight is a sustainable practice. Of course, if I've said that money can afford people freedom, that's where the side hustle likely comes in in the first place – but if it ends up taking up *all* your time, then you don't have the freedom to do the things you can now afford anyway. It's a balancing act, and one that each individual has to weigh up for themselves. In the end, my best advice is to remember that hard work is required to achieve, but smart hard work is the ideal.

Myth #8: I'm too old to start being better with money.

No, you're not. It's never too late to start changing financial habits. You're not an old dog, you can be taught new tricks. I've seen people in their sixties, seventies and beyond pick up *How to Be Good with Money* and say they have made changes in the way they manage their money that will stick with them forever. Granted, the most common comment I get from people in that age bracket is 'I wish I had you telling me this stuff 20 years ago' but they always find stuff they can change that has an impact on their finances.

One thing I often hear from people coming to the end of their working lives is that it's too late to start paying into pension. It's *never* too late to start paying into pension. In fact, I've worked with people who are just about to retire, have never paid into their pension, and we made a single contribution into one and it's still worthwhile.

Pension rules for people who work for somebody else or who are directors in their own company are based around what you take out of the pension. It works backwards. As a financial planner I can calculate what you're allowed to take out of the pension when you retire based on your age at retirement, your length of service with the company and your final salary. Once I know what you can take out, I can work out what the maximum is that you can put into the pension in order to provide that benefit. Now if the company has the willingness and the money to fund for that, they can actually put all that money in the day before you retire.

To put some numbers around this: a 60-year-old male with a 60-year-old wife with more than 20 years' service with a company and earning €50,000 could make a pension contribution of €1,053,000 just before they retire. Obviously if they own the company and the money is available they might do it. If they don't own the company, it's less likely that their employer would step up with this type of money just before they walk out the door. But the point I'm making is that it's never too late, if you have access to the money, to fund your pension.

Even if you're not getting close to anywhere near these numbers, it's still worthwhile investing in a pension as you approach retirement. If you have been working for a company for, let's say, 20 years and you have never paid into a pension, with 20+ years' service you'll be able to take out 1.5 times your salary as a lump sum. So if you earn €100,000, once there's enough in the pot you'll be allowed to get €150,000 out. With any lump sum, the first €200,000 is tax free and the next €300,000 is taxed at a special low rate of 20 per cent tax. Interestingly, the biggest detractor for pensions is often the fact that you can't get at the money until you retire. But if you're over the age of 60 and working, revenue rules say you can access your pension and continue to work. Your employer's rules for your scheme may be different but it *is* allowable under revenue rules. This means people can put money into pension in later life and know they are never too far away from getting it back if they need it.

For some people who have pensions from an old job, it's possible to access the pensions from the age of 50 onwards provided they no longer work for the company. People often ask me what they should do with an old pension from an old job. There are three options: leave it where it is; move it to the pension scheme of your new job or put it into a pension bond called a Personal Retirement Bond (PRB).

Leaving it where it is or putting it into a PRB are the best options. I don't really see the benefit of moving it to your new pension scheme in your new job. This is because it muddies the waters and it's impossible in the future to separate the pension from your old job and your new job because you have stuck them both together. This can cause problems with, for example, the withdrawal of lump sums. Leaving it in the old pension or moving it into a PRB in your own name, means that from the age of 50 you can take the benefits and keep working away (subject to pension scheme rules). Pensions are extremely beneficial from a tax perspective so obviously we try to leave pensions alone for as long as possible but it's nice to have that security blanket knowing that you can access the money in the pension from your old job if you need it.

As you get older, your financial focus can often shift. As you move from what we call in financial planning the 'accumulation phase' to the 'spending phase', it's useful to rain-check everything. The accumulation stage it when you're working away, building savings, pensions and other assets. The spending stage is the period where you're eating into it all and ideally enjoying life. Sometimes reviewing and changing how you handle your money at this point can have a dramatic impact on your overall enjoyment of your latter years and can often result in you having more money to enjoy. It can also highlight issues that might be coming down the tracks – like your offspring facing a hefty inheritance tax bill – so you either need to start spending more on yourself, giving more away or making moves to reduce the bill using other mechanisms.

Whether it's pension-planning or making changes to how you structure your finances or spend your money, it's never too late to start. There are different things to focus on as you get older but it's always useful to take the time to review your finances and it's never useful to stick your head in the sand

and either assume you know it all or, worse still, assume you can't make any improvements.

Myth #9: I'm too young to start being better with money.

You're never too old and never too young to look after your finances. The earlier the better, of course, but I still stand over the fact that it's never too late. But if you're young, don't let that comment make you think you can put things off.

Let me tell you about two friends, Jimmy and Johnny. At 22 years of age Johnny decides to put money into a pension. Let's say he decides to put in €1,000 per year. Jimmy is thinking, *I'm 22, I prefer pints to pensions.*

The years tick by with Johnny paying into a pension and Jimmy beginning to worry that maybe he should have too. But the worry isn't enough to get Jimmy started. Then they both hit 30: Johnny buys a house and stops the pension for what he thinks is a year or so until he gets settled into the house – but in the end Johnny never starts a pension again. All in all, Johnny pays a total of eight contributions of €1,000 each totalling €8,000 and stops putting money in from age 30 onwards.

Once Jimmy sees him stop he steps up and thinks, *Here's my chance to catch up.* From the age of 30 until the age of 65 Jimmy pays 36 contributions of €1,000 each, so a total of €36,000 into the pension.

When they reach retirement, Johnny, who only paid in €8,000 in total, has more money in his pension than Jimmy does, who paid in €36,000. In fact, given that Johnny and Jimmy are fictitious, let's assume a whopping 10 per cent growth on their pensions (which is unrealistic but helps me with the maths). Johnny ends up with a pension of over €350,000, while Jimmy ends up with a pension worth over €50,000 less than that even though he paid in four times as much in contributions.

Age	Johnny	Jimmy
22	€1,000	€0
23	€1,000	€0
24	€1,000	€0
25	€1,000	€0
26	€1,000	€0
27	€1,000	€0
28	€1,000	€0
29	€1,000	€0
30	€0	€1,000
31	€0	€1,000
32	€0	€1,000
↻	↻	↻
65	€0	€1,000
Total contributed	€8,000	€36,000

Compound growth is the young person's friend. Look at Warren Buffett: he is one of the richest men in the world, believed to be worth more than €100 billion as of mid-2021. It's well publicised that he started investing when he was 12 or 13 years old. He is now 91. But what is most incredible is that in 1982, when Buffet was 52 years old, he had a net worth of €376 million. That means that over 99.5 per cent of all of Warren Buffett's net worth today was accumulated after his 52nd birthday. Buffett is a great investor, with growth rates above 20 per cent in many years. There are other investors who achieved much better results but had nowhere near the longevity Buffett has and therefore never benefited as much from the compound growth effects.

Being young means you have time on your hands – use that time to your advantage. Compound growth is a powerful force and can be harnessed much better with youth. If you don't know what compound growth is, think about a snowball at the top of a hill: it starts to roll down, as it does it picks up more snow, more size, more pace and more power. Eventually it can't be stopped.

This is the same with your money: if you start small but early and let it build you get interest on interest and then more interest on that interest. Eventually you reach a point where, although relatively speaking your money is going up and down, no global financial crisis, Brexit or pandemic is going to destroy your wealth – provided of course you invest and forget.

Myth #10: The taxman is the only winner.

Grow up. Tax is part of life. The road you drove to work on was paid for with your taxes. The nurse who cared for your sick parent got their salary from your taxes. I have no issue with people complaining about how taxpayers' money is spent, but that is what your vote is for, so use it.

If you're paying tax you're making money. I'll stand down slightly and say I do know how it feels to pay tax and it can hurt. But the idea that you should in some way restrict your earnings so as to ensure you don't pay any more tax is probably the most perfect place for the use of the saying, cutting off your nose to spite your face.

I've seen people who are on the border of the higher-rate tax bracket. Every month their salary gets 20 per cent income tax plus USC (universal social charge) and PRSI (pay related social insurance) taken out of it – let's just say a round 30 per cent tax. Then they get a pay rise and it tips them into the higher rate of tax. So the extra €1,000 they're getting before tax turns into €500 after tax; and then they come to me and say, 'I never should have taken the pay rise/ new job/promotion, it isn't worth it for how much less I get to take home.'

Now if I'm asked this on radio or if I have a camera in my face when somebody comes out with this I'm going to be a bit more diplomatic in my reply. But given that right now I'm a keyboard warrior and this is my book, I'll tell you that at that moment I simply want to scream, 'Cop on!'

Yes, you have to pay more tax, but that is all part of growing up and progressing. What's the alternative – stagnate in your career, never take a pay rise and watch as the price of your groceries goes up and the purchasing power of your salary goes down? But well done you, you're not paying tax at the higher rate. These people are often the same people who complain about the rich getting richer and don't use the obvious tax breaks available to them like putting money into pensions and *reducing* their tax bill.

It always amazes me when I'm doing a corporate speaking gig in a room full of people and ask the question, 'Who's paying the maximum allowable into their pension?' and maybe a few hands go up. Then I say, 'Who wants to pay more in tax this year than they need to?' No hands go up, and I finish with, 'Who wants to pay less tax than they need to?' and all the hands go up. If you're not paying the maximum allowed into your pension this year then you're paying more tax than you need to this year. Simple. So don't complain to me about paying tax at the higher rate of tax until at very least you have maxed out your pension.

Myth #11: Next door has one …

'Those damn Joneses, we'll never keep up with them!' Guess what? You're right – so stop trying. You never know what's going on behind closed doors. The longer I spend getting to know people and getting to look under the bonnet of their finances, the more the message is driven home to me that everyone is on their own journey and people make decisions for different reasons all the time.

If you make your decisions because somebody else makes them, then they're not your decisions and you're trying to travel somebody else's journey. If you're looking at your neighbours and wondering *How come they can buy it and we can't?* then don't fool yourself. If it's a holiday, you have no idea what they went without to pay for that holiday. If it's an extension, you have no idea if they did it from savings or borrowing. If it's a car, that's the biggest joke of all – we don't have official figures because the area of car loans is not regulated – but from my own research I can tell you that more than 80 per cent of cars are financed. So at best, only 20 per cent of your neighbours are buying new cars from their savings; the rest are driving around in a new loan, not a new car.

I have gained a lot of insight from my clients granting me the privilege to look into their finances and discuss with them their hopes and dreams. I have come to the conclusion that cars, houses, boats, paintings, holidays, savings and pensions alone are not the secret ingredients to happiness. Yes, you need a certain level of financial security for true happiness, but your happiness does not grow exponentially with your balance sheet; and trying to make your balance sheet match your neighbour's without knowing what's going on in the background to create their balance sheet is a fool's game that will end in misery for you. Row your own boat.

Myth #12: I've never been any good with money.

You can change that. Keep reading.

Myth #13: There's always tomorrow …

Procrastination is your financial foe. I have seen it time and time again – people think to themselves that they will do something about their pension, savings and loans when things get better. Guess what? No one ever calls you to say, 'Things are better – now you can sort out your finances.'

Sometimes you need to take action now – and even if that action is very, very small, it's better than no action at all. Take savings, for example. You're either in the habit of saving or you're not. You decide. If you want to become a saver, just start. Start at a level so small that if you did not save that much money this month you would be mortified with yourself. The amount isn't important – it's the habit that's important. Once you have done it once and continue to do so, you're a saver and you have broken the habit. The biggest mistake I see people making when they become a saver is they go for it and go all in. Inevitably they save too much and have to dip into it or starve. This feels like a loss; you feel like you have failed. So I can't stress enough the importance of starting small, being consistent and building from there.

There is the story of the frog in the water. Before I start, I'll say no frogs were harmed in the making of this book! Anyway, if a frog is in a pot of water and you gradually turn the heat up under the pot the water will get warmer. If it's slow enough, the frog gets accustomed slowly and continues to swim around until eventually the pot reaches boiling point. By the time the frog realises, it's too late, and the frog is boiled alive. If the water was boiling from the start and the frog jumped in, it would immediately try to jump out again.

Think about the boiling water when starting any habit, but particularly when it comes to savings. Start at a really easy, gentle level and each time you get paid turn the volume up ever so slightly so you don't feel the pain. If one month you go a little too far too fast, then turn it down again until you're saving consistently each month without dipping into your savings.

Start your habit and don't procrastinate. I have seen so many people reach their late 50s, start to think about retirement and say, 'I just never got round to starting a pension.' Procrastination, particularly for long-term financial goals, can have a serious impact.

For example, keeping the maths simple, if at 60 years of age somebody puts €500 per month into a pension, by 65 they will have just under €35,000 in their pension pot. But if they had started ten years earlier and put in the same amount, a flat €500 per month, the amount in their pot would go up to €145,000. Now if that same person had started at the age of 30, putting the same flat €500 per month into their pension, they would have €712,000 in their pension when they reached 65. Starting 30 years earlier results in a pension pot 20 times bigger. Start at 20 and the pot will be almost 40 times bigger.

The price of procrastination	
Age you start	Pension pot at 65
20	€1,377,996.31
25	€995,745.37
30	€712,355.15
35	€502,257.52
40	€346,496.98
45	€231,020.45
50	€145,409.36
55	€81,939.67
60	€34,885.02
64	€6,167.78

Myth #14: Property is king.

In Ireland, we have a love of property. It makes sense: we can touch it, we can see it, in some cases we can even smell it. It's there and it's bricks and mortar. There is nothing hidden when it comes to property; there's no team of people sitting in some room somewhere deciding how to invest your money. A property is there in front of you, and you have full control and complete transparency – or do you?

If you already own property as an investment, I'm sure you'll agree that from time to time things go wrong and these things cost money. The boiler, the plumbing, the electrics, the fridge, whatever. It feels like you're finally getting ahead and you get hit with another bill of some sort. There is the advantage that when you're hit with these bills it feels very transparent: you can see a burst pipe, you can see the plumber working away on it and you see the bill they hand you for their hours – unlike pensions and investments, where you get a statement once a year and some charges which you kind of don't understand detailed on the statement.

When it comes to the cost of running a pension versus the cost of running a property, I would find it hard to see how the pension costs you more over time. When we buy property, we often have a biased view of the returns we get: we look at the fact that we put in the deposit of, let's say, €50,000 and then 30 years later we sell if for €500,000. That's €450,000 profit, right? Hardly. We forget about the mortgage we took out, the interest we paid, the plumbers, electricians and painters we paid over the years. We forget about the heartache we got from tenants and the hours we spent on the phone and in person dealing with issues. We also forget about the risk we took on by mortgaging ourselves up to buy it.

Let's look at the real numbers. I know of a house bought in Dublin in 1979: it cost £12,000, which converts to €15,270 at the time. Forty years later, in 2019, it was worth €500,000. These are actual numbers of a house I know well. This equates to a return of 9.11 per cent per annum, which by all accounts is very healthy. Add in the rent, assuming a yield of 5 per cent on average and your total return on the property is €790,142 over the 40 years.

But let's say that, like we did with Trump earlier, instead of buying this house in Dublin in 1979, we took the €15,270 and invested it in the US stock market (S&P 500 again) – over the same period you would have achieved a return of 11.705 per cent and your €15,270 would have turned into €1,278,626. I have ignored interest on the loan and the taxes on both the property and the investment, but still the difference is stark. If we started to consider all the paint, plumbing and sweat equity you would have had to put into the property over that 40-year period, it would only prove the worsening return we are getting for the property.

People might argue that investing 100 per cent of your money into the US stock market is very risky. But is it any riskier than buying one property, on one street, in one neighbourhood with one government deciding how many taxes and levies to hit you with and one tenant who can cause you no end of headaches?

The fact is most of our clients who have property as an investment start to offload it as they get older. The maths would suggest they should have done it sooner. We all like property because we can see it. But really when we delve into the numbers it does not make that much sense and I definitely think it's not worth the hassle. What does make property attractive is that a bank will lend you money, allowing you to dramatically increase your risk and so your returns. It will make the bank plenty of money too. Borrowing money is, quite rightly, not something many people would be comfortable with for the purpose of investing in the stock market, but somehow the same fear does not occur to them when investing in bricks and mortar.

Myth #15: Pensions are bad.

When I mention the word pensions at a public speaking engagement, it would not be unusual to hear a story about an experience somebody's mother, brother, friend or sister had where they lost all the money they had in their pension. The person telling the story will often go on to say that because of this experience they themselves would never touch a pension, and would be happier putting their money under a mattress.

Firstly, let's put the myth that pensions are bad to bed. Pensions are not bad. The thing people invest their pensions *in* or the advice that people get as to what to do with their pensions can be bad. In fact, countries around the world look at our pension structure with envy and wish they had similar set-ups. Yes, we could make some rules and breaks more attractive in places but what we have is excellent. It's just that not enough of us use them and this is simply because we either worry about putting money away today for the future, we don't worry enough about our financial future, we don't understand pensions or a combination of all of the above.

In their basic form, pensions are simply a savings plan with tax breaks and, no different to a savings plan, what you get out will be determined by what you put in. When you put money in the taxman gives a helping hand. So if you're on the higher rate of tax and put in €10 it will only cost you €6 because you'll pay €4 less in tax. In other words, it costs you €6 to put €10 into your pension. If you're on the standard rate of tax, it will cost you €8 to put €10. Once the money goes in, it grows tax free and then when you retire you can take a lump sum out (the first €200,000 of any lump sum is tax free and the next €300,000 is subject to a special 20 per cent tax). That one paragraph is all you need to know about pensions.

A pension is just a savings plan on steroids.

The reason pensions exist is because the government do not want you relying on them for money in your old age when you're no longer working, so they incentivise you using tax breaks to provide for yourself in retirement.

Pensions go wrong because of what they are invested in – the amount of people I have come across who were badly advised in 2006/7 to invest in bank shares such as AIB and Bank of Ireland! To be fair to the advisers, most of them worked for the banks themselves, most of them had lots of shares in those banks and none of them could have predicted the fall that was to come as a result of the global financial crisis. In addition, scratch the surface of any pension fund that was 'wiped out' and it was always as a result of an incredibly risky investment strategy that was seriously lacking in diversification and then a little bit of poor investor timing sprinkled on top to make things worse.

Saying you would not invest in a pension because somebody you knew lost all their money in a pension is, to me, the same as saying I would not eat food because somebody I know once got food poisoning.

The pensions industry likes to make the pensions world overly complex to create jobs for themselves. Yes, it's more complex than I have outlined here, yes there are other options to consider and other routes you can go with your pension but overall you get the idea. They are a good thing.

Myth #16: It is what it is …

This is such a defeatist attitude in life, never mind in money. We all know the person who feels the world is stacked against them, or worse, stacked entirely in their favour. These people won't try because they think there is no point. They don't believe they can change destiny and so they never try. Or else they believe there is no need to try because something magic is going to happen: they're going to get that big job, they're going to win that contract or buy that winning lotto ticket. These people always believe some financial knight in shining armour is just around the corner. It's not that there's no point in trying to change their finances today; there's no need to change their finances today because tomorrow is so much brighter.

Control your controllables! Your future hasn't happened yet and therefore you can't control it. What you *can* control is what you do with your money today. So change things, guide your destiny in the direction you want to go. Nobody else will do it for you.

In summary

There are lots of different opinions, methods, myths and beliefs about money and we can take something from all of them, whether that something is a good or a bad lesson. But we need to accept that being on top of our money and 'getting it right' can be boring. There's no secret; it's simple and it takes time. When we acknowledge that, we can truly learn.

Warren Buffett put it best: when asked why people don't just copy him to become as rich as he has, he said, 'Because nobody wants to get rich slow anymore.'

MONEY AND ME

Understanding our relationship with money can help us to improve our interaction with it and ultimately improve our outcomes. Once you have a handle on where your money goes and what you spend money on, the next step is to try and understand *why* you spend money. What are your drivers, what benefit do you get from it, what are you are trying to achieve when you spend? But also, how does earning money make you feel? How does it feel when you get a windfall, or if your income is less than expected in a particular month? Understanding what motivates your interaction with your money is when you can begin to implement real, lasting change.

Spending and saving

So, what makes us do the things that we do with money? What drives us to spend? What encourages us to save and what way do we feel when we do so? Having had countless consultations with clients where we ask them about their relationship with money, it's easy to recognise some very similar traits. People behave how they do for different reasons, but identifying in yourself why you spend money or save it can be extremely useful.

Spending money can serve many different purposes. Sometimes we must spend on essentials like food. Sometimes we need clothes and other times we might need to invest in a mode of transport, like a car. But what motivates us to go into artisan grocery stores, buy designer labels or go for expensive cars?

We will often try and convince ourselves that the reason we do it is *because of how it makes us feel*. I would say that is correct for about 15–20 per cent of people – they buy nice things because it makes them feel good about themselves. But I do think that, for most of us, it goes a little deeper. People – possibly unbeknownst to themselves – buy nice things to influence how others feel about them. We buy nice things so other people think nice things about us. And if other people perceive us in a certain way, this may in turn make us feel good about ourselves. If this were not the case for the vast majority of us then there would be no such thing as the fashion industry, and every car would look and cost the same – after all, the purpose of a car is simply to get you from A to B.

Once we acknowledge that when we buy stuff we are doing it to buy other people's opinions, then it can really help us to determine what we really want. I know some people will read this and tell me I'm wrong. I buy my expensive car every three years because it's reliable, I enjoy driving it and I like the brand: but the definition of a successful brand is that it creates a connection with a customer which is so strong that they are willing to pay more money than they would for a similar, cheaper one. Brands are designed to entice you into feeling loyalty towards them. If you don't believe me, question yourself about a recent purchase. Let's imagine you have recently bought an expensive German car. Now think to yourself and be honest – how would you feel arriving to your school reunion in that car? Now imagine a brand of car that is significantly cheaper and ask yourself how you would feel about arriving to the reunion in that car. Remember both cars served their purpose, both got you there. But if you're being truly honest with yourself, you felt differently about arriving in one versus the other. The only thing that changed was people's perception of you because you drove a different brand of car. Don't beat yourself up over this – it's what brands do and they are good at it.

Think about this: what people in your life actually matter? If you were broke, jobless and not feeling great about life, who would still come visit you six or even 12 months later? If you were terminally ill and could only speak to five people before you died, who would they be? Now think to yourself: do these people care what car you rock up in? If they do, are you sure you picked the right five people? People love you, not your car. The people who make judgements on you based on the car you drive or shirt your wear or type of avocado you buy don't actually matter at the end of the day. Think about them less and yourself more.

I'm saying this as somebody who drives a German car. There was a time when I was young and foolish and starting out in my career that I felt I needed a new car every couple of years or else clients would think I wasn't doing well. Then I got to the stage where I understood it made no financial sense to buy new cars and began buying two-year-old cars instead, where somebody else had taken the serious hit on the depreciation. I felt as a financial planner this was a good choice. I'll be honest – I haven't quite got to the point where I'm not buying nice cars but the time between each purchase is getting significantly longer and my obsession is becoming less and less with each purchase. But I accept I'm still learning and I'm still fighting what I know to be true and that is that a car is a silly thing to spend money on – but it's something I do enjoy!

The endorphin rush

Spending money often results in us feeling good and giving us a kick of endorphins. The problem is these endorphins can wane quickly and we have to go back for another hit. No different to popping a Pringle – and once you pop you can't stop – shopping is best prevented by not starting at all. On the TV show, I would often do an analysis of how much people are spending in different types of shops. One of the interesting figures I can often give the contributors is to tell them how much it costs them to go into a certain shop. So I'll say to them something like, 'I want you to realise that every time you walk through the door of X shop, it's going to cost you on average €23, so next time you're walking in tell yourself, this will cost me €23 and ask yourself, do I definitely want to go in?' Often it's as easy as me asking people not to go into the shop at all and we see dramatic reductions in their spending overall.

Getting the first hit leads to needing the second and too many hits can result in buyer's remorse. This is where you arrive home with a bag full of shopping, sit down and think to yourself, 'I just spent a fortune and I have no idea what I got.' The first thing to realise if you get a bang of buyer's remorse is that there is no shame in returning stuff. In fact, all the shame lies with you if you don't return it and it will keep visiting you every time you open your wardrobe to see the item of clothing you never returned hanging there with the tag still on it. Bring stuff back.

The best way to avoid buyer's remorse over non-essential shopping is to apply the same rules we use when going grocery shopping. Some of the top tips around grocery shopping are:

1. Don't do the supermarket shop when you're hungry because you end up buying much more.

2. Don't do the grocery shopping when you have loads of time, particularly if it's a quiet time in the shops. Shops play slow music at quiet times to slow you down and fast music when they are busy to speed you up and get more people through. If you have time and go at a quiet time you'll go through looking at everything and picking stuff up you don't need or want in the first place.

3. Don't do the grocery shopping without a list. A list means you buy with purpose and intent and you're more likely to stick to it.

4. Don't bring the kids or your partner if they are likely to mess with your routine, stick things in the trolley they want or generally stress you out or harass you for stuff you had no intention of buying. Remember shops are designed to take your money out of your pocket and put it into theirs. The more people with you, the more their marketing and store layout will have an impact.

5. Do a running total as you shop. Let's face it, we often walk away from the till scanning the receipt trying to figure out why our shopping cost so much. Counteract this by adding up the bill in your head as you put stuff into your trolley. The important thing is to be mindful.

Now if you could apply similar rules to your clothes shopping, it would dramatically help with your buyer's remorse and result in you shopping better. Obviously the rules need to be adapted – for example, going clothes shopping hungry mightn't be a bad thing in that without a full belly the clothes might fit better! I jest. In reality, shopping when you really need something can be very stressful and result in you buying more than you need so you can decide at home what works best. If you have loads of time to shop, it may result in you getting tired by the end of the day and not going back to first thing you saw and, instead, again buying more than you need.

Like using a list in the supermarket, the ideal way to shop for clothes is when you're looking for something specific. I love clothes shopping like this. If I know I'm looking for a blue jumper, for example, I can walk into a shop, scan it quickly and know they have nothing to suit and just leave. If I was just browsing, not knowing what I was looking for, I would end up looking at everything.

The more people who do your clothes shopping with you, the more opinions you'll get and the more likely you're to be influenced. Remember, having read the bit above, we should all be trying hard to please ourselves, nobody else.

Setting a limited budget when it comes to clothes shopping is the ideal. Decide before you go out how much you're going to spend and stick to it.

One extra rule you can apply is the 72-hour rule I've already mentioned, one of the core financial habits that everyone should try to employ: when you find something you want, put it back. If you still want it 72 hours later, then buy it. It was likely the right thing to buy in the first place but now you know it is. If you forget after 72 hours then you never wanted it in the first place.

Meaningful, conscious spending is good spending. It feels good. You won't have regrets or buyer's remorse and if you can practise it then it will mean you'll only buy things that add value to your life. It will cut out spending on things that don't add value, leaving more money for the things that do.

The saving bug

There are different reasons why we spend and there are different reasons why we save. Saving can often make us feel like we are taking control, empower us, make us feel confident about our future and secure if things go wrong.

Saving is a bug – it's just some people don't catch that bug until much later in life. I can think of so many people who have come to me and said, 'I have savings for the first time, I love it. I wish I'd done this years ago.'

When you think about it, saving money makes us feel grown up. It helps us to progress and allows us to make decisions about our money, meaning we control our money instead of our money controlling us. Building savings and having savings are two different things.

Don't ever underestimate the emotional attachment we have to our savings. If I meet somebody who has spent two years building a savings pot of €12,000 by saving €500 per month, those savings will mean so much more to them than if I meet somebody who was given €12,000, won it or it somehow dropped into their life. The person who built it over time knows the things they gave up each month to be able to save it. Maybe they moved home with their parents, maybe they missed weekends away with friends. Maybe they haven't brought the kids on holiday for two years. The fact is that building savings through sacrifice results in us having more of an attachment to those savings and I'm all for emotional attachment to our savings. In fact, I encourage it. One of the things I encourage is that you name your savings, as I mentioned on p61 – you're less likely to dip into the 'weekend away in August' fund than you are to dip into the miscellaneous 'rainy day' fund. Most banks will allow you to put a 'nickname' on your savings accounts. Use this facility: it reminds you every time you look at it why you're doing it.

This cropped up recently during an Insta Live when a couple wrote in: *Finally have money saved for honeymoon but now afraid to spend as we like our bank balance. Advice?*

My reply: *I love this! This happens all the time and it's exactly how you should feel. You now know it will only be spent wisely. A honeymoon is a one-off. Go and enjoy it but spend wisely without dampening the mood. You'll have savings again; you won't have another chance at a honeymoon – hopefully!*

Having a healthy attachment to our savings is natural. Thousands of years ago when we built walls, fences and castles around us we felt a bit safer. Today our personal security can be somewhat measured by our bank balance. Having savings reduces anxiety and helps us to make better financial decisions.

The problem is many people either never get to experience building and having savings or do so much too late in life. I recommend that you become a saver right now. It's easy and it's all relative: what might be a huge amount of money to you is nothing for somebody else, but guess what? It makes absolutely no difference because the benefits are relative. Start saving today by putting some money – any amount – to one side. I don't care how small and neither should you. Just start today and do it again the next time you're paid. You're now a saver. Once you're up and running then automate it – set up a standing order. You want to reduce your natural resistance by doing it automatically. Don't worry about the amount, just start small and then turn up the volume frequently.

Spending and saving causes a roller coaster of positive and negative emotions: each are equally beneficial and all your reactions are a learning opportunity. Recognising and owning these emotions is the first step in using them to your benefit. Being aware of how you feel about your money is a powerful tool.

Money personalities

We're often not great at getting in touch with our emotions, yet we identify with other people and their stories. I want to give you a few different examples of different personality types to help you identify your own traits and help you harness that knowledge for change in your finances.

First read through the questions below, then try to think about what your own response to each situation would be as you meet the money personalities. I've kept them simple; they are just hypothetical scenarios to get you thinking.

1. **You're coming to the end of a week away, and the holiday money you had budgeted for your trip is running low. Do you:**

   a) Stop spending immediately so that you have some money to go home with. Last night in the hotel room it is!

   b) What holiday budget?

   c) Work out exactly how much you now have left to spend each day, and make sure you stick to it.

   d) Keep spending as you had been, even if it means you have to put a few holiday treats on your credit card – sure isn't that what it's for?

   (a: Fionnuala Fear, b: Conor Clueless, c: Brenda Brilliant, d: Liam Later)

2. **Think back over your finances from the last five years. If you'd known then how well off you would be today, how would you have felt?**

   a) That your investments had worked out as you expected.

   b) That surely you could have done better.

   c) RELIEVED.

   d) You have no idea what state your finances are in, now or five years ago.

   (a: Brenda Brilliant, b: Gerry Greedy/Helen Hurry, c: Fionnuala Fear, d: Conor Clueless/Liam Later)

3. **Cryptocurrencies: where do you stand?**

   a) It's the next big thing, obviously.

   b) You're cautiously interested.

   c) How does it become real money, though?

   d) It doesn't seem very stable…

(a: Gerry Greedy/Helen Hurry, b: Brenda Brilliant, c: Conor Clueless, d: Fionnuala Fear)

4. **If your partner, your friend or a family member suggested a sit-down to go through all of your financial stuff, how would you react?**

    a) Fine, as long as they can do it quickly.

    b) You have a spreadsheet and a (short) presentation already prepared.

    c) Maybe next week?

    d) Delay, avoid, cut off all contact – you can't imagine anything worse.

    (a: Helen Hurry, b: Brenda Brilliant/Gerry Greedy, c: Liam Later, d: Fionnuala Fear/Conor Clueless)

5. **Your partner suggests employing a financial planner to get your money in order for the future. What is your first thought?**

    a) To be honest, you'd love to have someone else in charge.

    b) That … doesn't sound like something you would do.

    c) How much could they help – and how much would they cost?

    d) Sure, it's all online now. What will they actually be telling me?

    (a: Fionnuala Fear, b: Conor Clueless/Liam Later, c: Gerry Greedy, d: Brenda Brilliant)

6. **You have a lump of cash that's just sitting in your bank account; you don't need the money for another five years, so you decide to invest it long term. You engage with a financial planner and the money is invested appropriately on your behalf. Walking out of their offices afterwards, how are you feeling?**

    a) Excited about the potential profits.

    b) Eager to research the planner's strategy further – just to make sure there's nothing better out there.

    c) Glad that it's over with.

    d) Nervous – what if you lose it all?

(a: Helen Hurry/Gerry Greedy, b: Brenda Brilliant, c: Conor Clueless/Liam Later, d: Fionnuala Fear)

7. **You're working away with a set salary when your boss offers you new terms for the same job: your base rate will be cut in half, but you'll now earn commission on whatever sales you make. If your sales continue as they have done for the past three years, this will mean a 50% pay rise from when you were non-commission based. Do you take your boss's offer?**

a) Absolutely – where do I sign?

b) Absolutely not – it's far too much of a risk.

c) Say that again?

d) You'll need to think about it.

(a: Brenda Brilliant/Helen Hurry/Gerry Greedy, b: Fionnuala Fear, c: Conor Clueless, d: Liam Later)

It's worth noting that these characters have been simplified; real people are regularly a mix of these personalities, or switch between types at different stages of their lives. So don't overthink it! Whether you recognise yourself in one character or all six, this is to help give you a jumping-off point for understanding your financial mindset and the common pitfalls that may apply to each personality type.

Fionnuala Fear

Fionnuala is terrified about how things will be in the future. She worries whether she'll be able to pay for bread and milk in 30 years' time. She worries whether she'll ever clear the mortgage. She worries about whether or not she'll be able to support her kids and this worry then leads her on to worrying about whether her kids will ever be able to support themselves. How will they ever buy a house? Will they always have to rely on her? Strange thing is, Fionnuala doesn't have kids. But as she says herself, *Yeah but what if I do some day?*

Strangely, although Fionnuala worries a lot about money, she doesn't stress at all about everything else in her life. She is a happy-go-lucky-type gal, rides a motorbike, jumped out a plane last year and she is somebody her friends turn to for advice all the time. She's in a stable relationship and has a good job. It's just money she worries about – oh and the kids she hasn't had yet.

So why is it that money causes Fionnuala to worry so much? The reality is that money causing stress is not unusual. Research by the American Psychological Association from 2015 found that 54 per cent of respondents said money is their biggest stress. To put that in perspective, the next biggest category was work at 18 per cent, followed by 12 per cent of people stating it was their relationship.

So why does Fionnula allow money to rent space in her head and cause her so much anxiety when everything else in her life is fine? It's a combination that comes down to several things including the fact that she has lost her way a little and she is not using her money to add value to her life. She hasn't identified this yet and it's causing her unease. Maybe she knows she's not taking care of her long-term financial future properly, the likes of her pension. This is a concern for Fionnuala and, until she addresses that issue, she will always feel wrong about what she spends day to day and worry about it excessively.

But having spent time with a number of Fionnualas, I believe I know the root cause of their problem. You see, Fionnuala has made some stupid decisions in the past around money. She invested some money in something she didn't check out first and lost all the money in what turned out to be a scam. This was her biggest mistake, but she has had other minor blunders along her financial journey and is now in a position where she has no confidence in her ability to make the right decisions around her money. This means she tries to avoid making decisions in case she gets them wrong. This causes a cycle and the stress elevates.

To restore her confidence, she first needs to start making some financial decisions. She needs to accept some will go right and some will go wrong. Ideally she should work with somebody or at very least talk to her partner and ask for their help in making decisions. This is something Fionnuala has been reluctant to do up to now because she feels a little stupid. She shouldn't; they didn't teach this stuff in school.

Gerry Greed

Gerry is greedy. When I say the word 'greedy', people often think of the likes of Scrooge. But greed goes well beyond just the image we have of Scrooge hunched over his desk writing with his quill. Gerry has lots of money and wants more. When you go into his house he has the best of everything and when you open his press he has more in there than any one person or family could possibly get through during the food's shelf life.

When I talk to Gerry, he can't quite put his finger on why he has this obsession with money and why he has need to have more of it. But is this a bad thing? Is greed something we should all look down on or is something to be encouraged?

We live in a society that believes in the idea of growth and progression. None of us truly believes the future, particularly our long-term future, is going to be worse than our life today. We expect things to get better and we expect things to grow and progress. This includes how much money we have. As a bank manager once said to me when I handed him a business plan, 'I have never seen a bad set of projections.' This is true. We never project the future to be miserable.

Gerry is just feeding into that. He wants the future to be better so watching his bank balance grow helps him see that future growth today and he gets something from that. To me greed is healthy, up to a point. We all know too much of anything is not good for us. Too much food makes us unhealthy, too much drink gives is a sore head. But how much money is too much?

As a society we tend to frown upon the person with 'too much money'. 'That display of wealth is disgusting' or the amount of money that soccer player is paid is 'immoral, it's just wrong'. Where does that come from? Why as a society do we accept the concept of progress and growth but deny it when one person excels at it? I think it's rooted in our ancestry. All of our ancestors came from a time when resources were limited. They all had to eat the crop from the same field or share the same resources. If one person got more than another person, then it meant one person had less. When you have finite resources, when the pie is only so big, then somebody taking more than their fair share feels very unfair to the rest of us. Although we have evolved and although most people would have no clue how much money there is in the world today, i.e. how big our money pie is, we still feel that if somebody has more than us that somewhere along the line we are going to lose out as a result.

But Gerry's greed could be healthy – in fact, we all need a little greed to fuel progress. If every company was paid exactly the same amount of money for their widgets, regardless of how many they produced, then there would be no incentive to make better widgets or more of them. There would be no incentive to introduce efficiencies and cuts costs and improve because you're being paid the same regardless of your output or your quality. So why bother? So we do need greed. But if Gerry is greedy to the point that he won't spend his money in fear of how it would make him feel, then it's a problem. But that is not the case with Gerry: he has lovely things, he spends his money but he has a possibly healthy obsession with accumulating more, that's all.

Gerry's issue is that he doesn't know the answer to one simple question: how much is enough? He doesn't know when to stop. He doesn't know how much money he needs to be able to live the life he wants to live for the rest of his days. Thankfully there is an easy fix to this – it may sound like a plug, but this is what financial planners were put on this earth to do. When I sit down with a private client, ultimately 'What is enough?' is the question we're answering. Do you have enough money already to live the rest of your life the way you want to live it? If you're not there already, when will you get there? What age will you be? Then finally if we make changes to how you manage your money, will you get there any sooner?

If Gerry went through this process with us today, we could tell him whether he has reached his point of financial independence, i.e. the point in life where he has created enough wealth that he does not have to work again and he does not have to worry about money. If he is already there, it's likely he reached it sometime in the past because it would be one serious coincidence if he happened to walk into my office on the same day that he reached financial independence. So if he reached it in the past, it's likely he has more money than he needs. We can tell him how much extra he could spend and still not run out of money before he reaches the age of 100. We can also test to see what happens to his money should the economy fall apart and cause a temporary decline in stock markets.

If Gerry went through this process with us, we could also tell him how much cash he still needs to reach financial independence. This can really be interesting for business owners in particular. Imagine Gerry had his own business, he has not yet reached financial independence but we do analysis and we figure out that if he sold the business and got, let's say, €800,000 from the sale he would never have to work again, he would be financially independent. Gerry also talks to his accountant and they value the business at €1 million. Gerry is feeling good about things.

The conundrum comes, however, when an offer comes in for the business. Somebody wants to buy Gerry's business and the offer is €900,000. Now Gerry's accountant is telling him that the business at that price is undervalued by 10 per cent. We, however, are telling Gerry that if he takes that money he has surpassed financial independence, he will have enough money to never have to work again, do all the things he wants to do and still have some surplus left over.

We're recommending he takes the money. In this case €900,000 is more than 'enough'.

This is where Gerry's true test of greed comes in. Does he listen to his accountant and hold off at the risk of losing the buyer or does he take the money and run, knowing he left some on the table but personally he got everything he needs to live happily ever after?

Gerry just needed to know how much was enough. He listened to us and took the money.

Helen Hurry

Helen wants it all, but Helen wants it all right now. Helen is that person next to you at the lift that presses the button four or five times before the lift arrives, somehow using her magic ability to make it come faster. She is the person behind you at the traffic lights who beeps at you, twice, because you were turning on the aircon in the car and missed the fact that 4.5 seconds ago the light went green. Helen is in a hurry.

Helen's heightened level of anxiety is rooted in the concept of fight or flight. When in danger, we will react by fighting or running away, depending on which option intuitively seems to present the best outcome for our survival. This is really useful if you're alone in the woods and you meet a bear. But financially it's less of a friend. You see, Helen is constantly trying to catch the next big thing, she's constantly worrying she's going to miss out. She may take big risks to get to her financial goals quicker and when she does, she often doesn't allow her investments the time they need to succeed because they are not moving fast enough for her. She suffers dreadfully with FOMO (fear of missing out) and any time I make investment recommendations to her she thinks they are boring, stale and too safe. But what Helen is looking for are big returns with no risk. When I answer a call from Helen I'm just waiting to hear about her next hare-brained ideas about how to get rich quick that she heard from somebody not qualified to come up with the idea, never mind be advising others to put money into it.

Helen is one of those clients who are almost impossible for a financial planner to deal with. If they come to you with a madcap idea and you tell them to go with it and it blows up, then it was my fault. But if I tell her not to go into something and her friends do and it goes brilliantly, then what type of financial adviser am I that I couldn't spot a good thing when I saw it?

In my private practice we deal with people like Helen by only investing clients' money and pensions in boring stuff that works and has lasted the test of time. It won't necessarily excite them but it will never make them lose sleep at night either. We build the financial plan around these 'boring' options and we take a more conservative approach than our peers with regard to future growth. Doing it this way means that we have every confidence in that plan working.

The difficulty with dealing with Helen is that she doesn't see the long game. She lives for right now and wants everything in the moment. She wants excitement and wants to be able to say she bagged a big one. It would be easy for me to suggest that what Helen needs to do is get her thrills from some other aspect of her life: take up sky-diving or rock-climbing, Helen, and allow your money to be the boring part of your life!

The only way to help Helen is to let her learn from herself. Helen arrived to my office because of something we see all the time: her partner wanted our help to try to get us to change her ways. But that's never what is said, we just pick up on it. He has been trying for years to calm her down financially and we are often the last-ditch attempt to get it sorted and protect the family's financial future.

Helen arrived to us having had serious success with her business ventures, I'll absolutely give her that. She had successfully built and sold more than one business and was excellent at doing it. The issue now – and the reason her partner had her in the room with us – is because she was now taking a break from the day job and had decided that her excellence and confidence were transferable skills to the world of investing. She had some early wins, which compounded her belief in her abilities. When we started to present data to her about how she was investing in very focused shares in companies that were only in one sector or industry, she didn't like the challenge. Despite the data in front of her proving that it was luck she'd had the first couple of wins, she still felt we did not know what we were talking about. As we challenged some of her beliefs, her partner would jump in from time to time with a little 'did you hear that' or 'see?' It was evident we were there to lead the charge for the partner who wanted things to change.

Ultimately Helen continued doing her thing; then she disappeared for a while. She would be busy whenever we called and cancelled some of our meetings. This rarely happens in our private practice and, when it does, alarm bells ring. Initially I felt she had the hump and we had got the balance wrong. We had pushed too hard and insulted her and her self-confidence. But then I managed to get hold of her. She started with, 'You were right, I'm not a day trader, I don't know how to pick shares and I need to pass the reins over to you to manage the money.' She had lost money, a lot of money. It was a hard lesson to learn but ultimately it was salvageable and she had to work for a couple more years despite having previously reached financial independence.

With someone like Helen, we usually suggest they set up a bingo bucket, typically 10–15 per cent of their investable assets. They manage that, invest in whatever they want, and we manage the other 85 per cent in the boring, stable way we do. Over time, our 85 per cent will grow to 100 per cent anyway, so even if they lose all the 15 per cent we will replace it.

Inevitably what happens at our first annual review meeting is that their 15 per cent has done incredibly well and our 85 per cent is lagging behind. They want more of the pot to play with. It's at this point the partner jumps in, puts their foot down and says no.

People like Helen need to learn by themselves, often the hard way. But they also need to decide how to introduce excitement into their lives. And guess what, Helen – money isn't exciting. Life is.

Liam Later

Liam is really nice, a little bit scatty when it comes to his finances but focused and successful in every other aspect of his life. He has a stellar career, so the organisational issues only relate to his finances.

Liam is great at making money. He has a high-powered executive role and is great at accumulating money. The issue with Liam is that whenever I ask him to do something with his finances it's always, 'Yes Eoin, I'll definitely do that … Later.' He'll then not fill out forms, not send them back, miss deadlines and then start the entire routine again the next time we meet. I'm not joking: I've dealt with Liam for 10+ years and he is always lastminute. com with his annual pension contribution and on one occasion missed the deadline altogether despite our very best efforts.

Initially I took his lack of response as being my fault. I thought I was handling the situation badly. Let's face it, traditional financial advisers were a pushy bunch. It was all about high-pressure sales tactics. It was bad for what was then an industry (and not the profession that financial planning is today) but more importantly it was bad for the client. I came into financial planning when it was being better regulated but some rogue elements still exist. It's not unusual for a new client to say to me, 'I do have an adviser but it always feels like they're trying to sell me something.' As a result I tend to go the other way completely: we don't sell products, we help clients buy them. I know that's a play on words but it's so important to me and the difference is significant.

Although I was afraid of being too pushy, the reality is that Liam is a procrastinator. And when people procrastinate, it's usually out of a fear of something, sometimes because they don't understand what they are doing. Another reason for procrastination is that people believe they don't have the ability to complete the task so by not doing it they have no chance of failure. This is a classic scenario. Some people would rather not try so as never to fail as opposed to others who know that it's – to coin the phrase – better to have tried and failed than never to have tried at all.

But Liam was more straightforward than all of this. He just wasn't worried enough about his future to do something about it today. He was making great money, he could see his bank balance and he simply did not have the brain space or motivation to do anything about fixing it all because it has always worked out in the past.

We got around this by consistently, year on year, showing him the positive benefits of his past actions. We would show him the money he invested versus the money he had left in his bank account and how his pension and investments were working so much harder. Typically as a financial planner you're mapping out the financial future so people are motivated towards it. Liam was not worried about his future, but he did appreciate hard work. When we could show him how much harder his money worked for him if he filled out the pesky forms, it motivated him. In this case, looking backwards instead of forwards did the job.

If you procrastinate, try to get to the bottom of why you do it. Is it too hard, are you worried about failing or could it be you just don't know how to tackle your finances? Identifying the problem in this instance is more than half the battle.

Conor Clueless

You've got to love Conor, sailing through life with few or no cares in the world, clueless to his past financial mistakes and not really worried about what his financial future looks like either. Conor doesn't even know what a tracker mortgage is.

That's fine, provided Conor is not having us all on. We've had Conor clients in the past. He'll have this *I don't have a care in the world, I just live for today and I don't want to learn about this stuff because it bores me*-type attitude. But when we actually spend 20 minutes in a room with him looking at his financial situation and his financial future, he looks completely petrified.

You see, Conor is often the reluctant partner who is brought along because 'We're in this together, we're a couple'. Conor's partner wants him to grow up a bit and take some responsibility. Conor's partner is often the one who manages the family finances and does all the worrying so Conor can sit back without a care in world spending money and not understanding what the big deal is – sure, there's loads of money in the account.

His blissful ignorance is a nice place to be. But those petrified eyes tell a different story. What we discover is that Conor actually does care – he's just sticking his head in the sand so that he is never asked to take the financial reins. This is an unfair place for Conor to put his partner in and, over prolonged periods of time, will cause friction in any relationship.

When Conor comes to our office, we get him interested by bringing the abstract money stuff closer to real life. We do this with all our financial plans, but it's particularly important that we highlight it with a Conor. What I mean by this is that a financial plan is simply a road map detailing what you should do with your money today and into the future to ensure your money supports the life you want to have.

A Conor-type person is often taken aback that our questions are mostly being directed at them. We ask them what they want to do, where they want to go in life. We ask them to dream. We then show them how to achieve it financially. When you're telling Conor that if you do this it's going to be the Caribbean in the future and if you don't do this it's going to Cork (I love Cork, promise), then Conor listens.

If you genuinely struggle to understand financial stuff, go learn about it. Sit with a professional. If after sitting with a professional you still don't understand, then I suggest you went to the wrong professional. This stuff is not complicated, it just needs to be properly communicated. Don't ever feel stupid because someone isn't explaining something properly.

Brenda Brilliant

We all know a Brenda. They do everything right, they know everything and unfortunately sometimes they can't be told. But Brenda listens – I know this because she often challenges things I say by telling me what other people have said. So she does listen.

If you're a Brenda, you're going to struggle to accept what I'm about to say, but please do let it sink in if you can. Brenda is a know-it-all and does everything right because underneath it all she is a perfectionist. And Brenda is a perfectionist because she actually suffers with inadequacy issues or fears disapproval. Think about it: if you worry what others think of you, then you'll try to do something perfectly to ensure it meets with those others' approval.

When it comes to your finances, you don't need perfect. I remember once visiting the Facebook offices in Dublin. It's incredible in there: free food, free sweets, beanbags and places to chat to your colleagues. I remember describing the visit to my brother Mick afterwards, how the vibe in the place was relaxed yet professional. (He remarked that Facebook was the only company in the world where, when your boss walks up behind you, you close down Excel really quickly and open up Facebook!) But the thing I feel Brenda could learn the most from was a slogan on one of the walls at Facebook that said: *Done is better than perfect.* When I asked my host about it, they explained that it's a bit of a motto in there: get something finished and it will be 95 per cent right and workable, but getting the last 5 per cent done to reach perfection is not worth the time and effort.

Brenda could take this on board and realise that not even one of the most successful companies in the world strives for perfection. For them, done is good enough. For us dealing with Brenda, we learned that the best way to get her on board was to make it *her* idea. A perfectionist always believes that if you want something done right, then do it yourself. So we would plant the idea in her head and then let her feed it back to us minutes, hours or weeks later as her own idea.

I get that this is a slightly simplistic approach, but if you're a financial perfectionist you need to load yourself up with sufficient knowledge about what it is you need to do in order to feel comfortable and execute whatever financial decisions you're pondering.

Who are you?

Having now met the money personalities, it's time to decide which one you are. The questions at the start of this section were designed to help you think about financial situations and how you tend to react to each one, but of course there's a spectrum rather than an absolute answer. No doubt as you were reading through, you recognised yourself and maybe other people you know, or even just individual traits; but try to rank how close you are to each personality. Then try listing the pros and cons of the personality closest to you. The aim here is to think more deeply about your current financial mindset – and how this could benefit you, but also where you may be more likely to fall down.

Think about each of the characters, ask yourself who most resonates with you and what can you learn from that. I hope it came across that there is no right or wrong or good or bad personality types. Each presents its own unique challenges and opportunities but, most importantly, each gives us something to learn from. Once you have identified with one of the personality traits, what should you learn from it and, more importantly, what should you change so that you get all the strengths and fewer of the 'weaknesses' related to that trait?

For the **Fionnualas** out there, the first thing to realise if that no amount of worry about anything in the past will change the outcome. We have inbuilt fear – a fight-or-flight instinct that stopped us being eaten by lions. It's useful to have and in current times probably our biggest defence against our own in-built stupidity. We need to recognise our fears when they appear. But it's what we do next that is important. Our bodies tell us to be fearful so that we can make an adjustment and improve a potentially bad situation. I saw a great comment from author James Clear recently on Twitter, which sums up exactly what you need to do about your finances if you're constantly worrying about them: 'Working on a problem reduces the fear of it. It's hard to fear a problem when you're making progress on it, even if progress is imperfect and slow. Action relieves anxiety.'

Take the word 'problem' and replace it with the word 'finances' and all of a sudden you have the perfect recipe for fixing any fears you have around your money. Get yourself informed about your current position, get a clear picture of where you're going and build your knowledge by reading books like this and you'll be in a much better place. The positive of being a Fionnuala Fear is that ultimately the fear will drive you closer to fight and away from flight, but only if you direct it that way.

If you are worried your partner or your mates might find out you're a **Gerry**, then do not despair. Remember, greed can be healthy. Without it none of us would progress, develop or grow. We need a healthy level of greed to keep us moving forward. You having more money than your neighbour does not prevent them from growing their own bank balance, or vice versa.

Recognising your 'greed' is important so you can use it to harness your drive. But do check yourself from time to time and, just like with all the other personality traits, ask yourself regularly, is my behaviour working for my benefit or against it? If you're finding that you're going without things that bring you enjoyment just so you don't have to dip into your savings, then push yourself to answer the question: what's it all for?

You're building this money, but for what purpose? We know having more money in itself does not make us happier – it's what the money can do for us, the experiences and security we get from having money that the happiness stems from. So from time to time you should be asking yourself what your money is doing for you – and if the answer is not a lot, then take corrective action like spending some to remind yourself what it's all about. Equally you should be harnessing the good in greed to spur yourself on, so if you believe you share none of Gerry's traits, then maybe it's time to instil some greed into your life.

As for **Helen Hurry** ... I know I said there are positives and negatives in all of these traits, but I'll be honest, this one challenges me a little to find the positives. If you see a lot of Helen in yourself, then the biggest positive is the fact that you recognise it in the first place. Please just slow down – our lives are run at 100 mph but we can all benefit from taking a breather occasionally. When it comes to finances, good things come to those who wait. Accept you have a long life ahead of you, and no matter how old you are or how old you feel, it's never too late to make positive change to your financial future.

Yes, there are positives in wanting everything to happen quickly – you'll be spurred on to make change and it will give you drive – but a positive impact on your finances comes from doing small things repetitively and achieving huge results over longer periods of time. When you start to think like a financial planner, you realise that your financial plan is from now until you're 100 years of age – and unless you're 99, that is a very long time from now. You have time. Just slow down.

The next time you're jumping into something financially, clock it and stop it. Just take a step back. *I do need to make a decision, but do I need to make it this instant?* It's no different to the person who likes to shop: apply the 72-hour rule to your financial decisions.

If you feel closer to **Liam Later** then the first step is to identify what is making you procrastinate in your financial decision. It could be a fear of filling the forms out incorrectly; it might be that you don't understand what it is you're doing, or maybe you're worried that leaving your finances as they are is actually where they should be and making no changes is better than making a change for the sake of it? Or perhaps you just don't get on with your personal adviser, in which case move on to another one.

Remember when you start to look at your finances, it would be incredibly unusual for you to have everything set up perfectly, so change will likely be needed. You'll need to make a decision. You don't actually avoid a decision by doing nothing, so accept that doing nothing is a decision. *It's a decision to do nothing.*

Once you own the fact that a decision has to be made, whether that is to change stuff or to decide to do nothing, you're on the hook to actually make a decision. So satisfy yourself as to why you're procrastinating and try to resolve it to a point where you're comfortable.

For all the Liams out there, I have one silver bullet to help you through. A deadline. Ideally get your partner or your adviser to give you one and agree with them that by a certain date you'll have the decision made to stick or twist.

First of all, I can hazard a guess that you're not a **Conor Clueless**. Conor does not pick up, buy and read books about money. It's more likely someone you know is a Conor. Either way the treatment for the cluelessness is the same.

You've got to bring the money to life. Next time you're about to buy something for €80 don't think of it as €80 – think of the money in terms of time. To keep it simple, if you earn €10 an hour then it's not €80, it's eight hours' work. Next time you're thinking of putting money into savings, then have a goal; a vision for what those savings are going to do. 'I'm putting €100 per month away for 12 months so I have €1200 in a year's time to go to a beach in Spain for a week.'

Changing your financial actions today into relatable visions of the future is what you need to do so that the inner Conor in you becomes interested, engaged and excited.

And as for the **Brendas** – well, Brenda, you're brilliant. You have an amazing ability to garner information from all types of different sources, process it, understand it and then what helps you is that you spit it back out again as your own idea.

When a Brenda is in my office, it's a wonderful challenge for me as a financial planner, because here I am with 20+ years of experience dealing with client's finances and I'm effectively being schooled as to why my approach is wrong or being told why Brenda has a better way. I welcome this, and to be honest we all need Brendas in the world to collate information and challenge how things are done.

But if you're a Brenda, please do know your limitations. I love when a client goes off and gathers information, but I also love when the same client is willing to accept an evidence-based retort about what they learned in a 90-second YouTube video. I want you to gather all the information you can and then be open to suggestions about how you could improve on your methods. But most importantly of all, recognise that the people in the finance world are on your side. They are working *with* you to get you better financial outcomes and you're going to them for their expertise, knowledge and experience. All I ask is that, as a Brenda, you challenge but also listen.

Recognising your personality type allows you to use your traits to your advantage. Equally our money personalities can and do change over time. But most important of all is realising we can choose to change how we are with money – we just need to know how.

THE PRACTICALITY
OF MONEY

When you start to think about your financial future and what you want it to look like, you must first get a clear picture of where you are today. People who have a financial planner have 2.5 times the net worth of people who don't when they reach retirement. We have already discussed why this might be, but one thing a financial planner does is that they force you to regularly check your finances. Having a planner means you have a third-party review of your current position on an annual or bi-annual basis.

This is important: it's a frequent reminder of where you were, where you are now and where you are going. I couldn't count the amount of times we take on new clients and they are paying, let's say, €500 per month into their pension. When we ask why that sum is €500 and how long has it been €500, the answer is invariably, 'It's just always been like that, I don't know why we choose €500 per month, it was years ago.'

€500 per month may have been the right amount 11 years ago when they set the plan up, but things change, salaries increase and expectations for retirement change. If these clients had been engaging with a planner on a regular basis, the payment would have been kept up to date and relative.

If you decide not to engage a planner, do yourself a big financial favour, follow the process I outline below and when you have done it, put a reminder in your phone to do the entire process again this time next year. At least then you have some hope of things being kept up to date, you have less chance of losing anything and you won't wake up in ten years' time thinking, *I wish I'd kept a closer eye on this stuff.*

So when looking at you finances, where should you start?

1. Identifying where you are

With financial planning, what's happened in the past is useful to know but where you are today is a reflection of all your previous financial decisions. Financial planning is about the future; the past is not irrelevant but nothing can be done about it now so it's not somewhere we should expend too much energy.

When looking at where you are today, you should first take a piece of paper. Draw a line from top to bottom, straight down the middle and then another in the middle of the page from right to left. You now have four quadrants. Write in the top left the word *Own,* top right *Owe,* bottom left *Earn* and bottom right *Spend,* just like I've done opposite:

You could do this in Excel or Word, but I would suggest you don't go there just yet – stick to the paper for now. Next you need to start filling it in. This is your first shot so don't worry too much about accuracy. For example, if you have roughly €160,000 left on the mortgage just put in €160,000 for now. You don't want to be distracted at this stage by having to go off to find your most recent statement. The process needs to be quick, off-the-top-of-your-head stuff, so we build a reasonable picture of where you are before you lose interest or get distracted.

Own	Owe

Earn	Spend

If you're struggling to understand what goes in each area, here are some examples to spur you on:

Own	Owe
Car	Car loan
House	Personal loan
Pension	Mortgage
Savings	Family loan
Bank accounts	Credit card
Credit union	Overdraft

Earn	Spend
Salaries	Utilities
Overtime	Groceries
Side hustle	Entertainment
Child benefit	Holidays
	Loans
	Car
	Medical

Remember, I don't want you to get too bogged down at this stage. For example, when it comes to your expenses, writing in one figure that covers everything will suffice. The expenditure list will be done separately, later in the process. If this process takes you longer than 15 minutes, then you're going into too much detail. The purpose here is to start you thinking. It will remind you of what stuff you need to go off and get the details on and it will very quickly give you an idea of your net worth.

Net worth is the amount of money you would have in your back pocket if you sold everything you owned, cleared off your loans and headed for Rio. You'll get yours by adding up everything in box 1 and deducting everything in box 2. Net worth is a useful gauge for me as a financial planner: people can take home a very high wage but also incur very high expenses and therefore as I revisit their net worth each year I can see they are not actually adding value. People can also have lower salaries and low expenses and have a positive increase in net worth each year.

Once you have your figure, you now have a rough benchmark. Do this once a year and you'll start to build a course and can measure your progress or identify if you're going backwards.

The reason I want this to be done quickly is because I want you to get a quick win. I want you to find out what your financial picture looks like today, but it also gives you a map of what your finances look like. Next, I want you to get the finer details on everything. Look down your list in boxes 1 and 2: do you have recent statements on everything in the boxes? If you do and you know exactly where they are, pull them together. If you don't know exactly where they are, don't go off on a wild-goose chase – just send a few emails instead. If you don't have all the details in the house, then you need to contact each of the life companies and pension houses. In our private practice, one of our services is to do this on behalf of clients. It's very straightforward: clients give us a written authority to allow us gather the information. We then write to each company and ask them to provide details. My suggestion for you is to simply ask for the most recent 'benefit statement', typically a one-pager, which provides a summary of the policy and will be more than sufficient to fill out your boxes in more detail. Once you've done this, it's a great record for you to have. It's also really useful for others if the worst were to happen to you and they wanted to start tracking down your assets.

But I don't want you to fire off the emails now to gather the information and then park the idea of filling out the form until everything comes back – we're on a roll now so let's not lose momentum. (And if you really struggled on the expenses box, jump back to it now and try to jog your memory so that you can add more details.)

2. Identifying where you want to go

Once you have a reasonable picture of where you are today, it's time to start thinking about what you want for yourself in the future. Really think about what you want to do in the short term and what you want to do in the long term. We ask people this every day and it's really interesting to see the things people want to plan for financially. It's also essential that your goals are yours: if you're in relationship it's important that you have shared goals – there's no point in one of you going off planning your dreams and goals and financial future if the other one is in the dark about it all.

Some of things we see people plan for in the short term are:

 ▷ Get out of crappy debt

 ▷ Pay for holiday using savings not a loan

 ▷ Build a buffer

 ▷ Buy a car

 ▷ Move out

Longer-term goals tend to be along the lines of:

 ▷ Financial security

- ▷ Retire early

- ▷ Second property

- ▷ Get kids through college

- ▷ Deposit for a house for the kids

- ▷ A boat

- ▷ A year out of work

- ▷ The Camino

- ▷ Family trip

- ▷ A big sport occasion like the Lions' tour, the Ryder Cup or to run the Tokyo marathon

As I said, it's important to choose your own goals. Once you have your list, then it's time to test how important they are to you and your partner, if you have one. Look across both your long- and short-term goals and rank them all. Put a 1 next to the one that is an absolute must. It's important that you're honest with yourself and, if you're in a relationship, that you listen to each other and both agree the priorities. This part of the process can be really interesting as it can often throw up some fascinating discussions when one person realises just how important something is to somebody else or to themselves.

When prioritising the goals, remember that we will often be more attracted to the 'nice' ones, but it's not just about doing the nice things. The practicalities are important too. For example, getting out of debt is difficult but if you do it then it facilitates all the other 'nice' things you want to use your money for.

When you have your priorities sorted, it's really useful to complete the boxes again in more detail. You then need to explain how your spending reflects your goals. Are you currently spending on your values or are they out of sync? Get the balance right – often this process alone can allow you to refocus your spending to be more in line with your goals.

You'll need to identify some money to put towards your goals, so go through your expenses and see where it can come from. Cut costs where possible: do the easy stuff like changing utility provider and addressing the big stuff like the mortgage. Could you save money there?

Remember, you're identifying your goals here and achieving them is going to require you doing something different with your money from now on. Identify what money you have available to put towards these goals. Start by cutting spending on things that don't align with your goals and values.

3. Bringing future goals into today

Once you have your goals prioritised and you have identified some money, you need to start to work on them. Ask yourself, *What do I need to do today to reach my goal?* Some will be easier to address than others. For example, if you want to go on holiday in 12 months' time and you want to pay for it from savings, then work out how much money you need. If you think €1,200 will do it, then right now, today, put €100 into a separate account and do that every month for the next 12 months. If you can't afford to put €100 per month away, then guess what? You can't afford that holiday. It's that simple. I find for these short-term goals that using the fintech banks like Revolut, N26 or An Post Money is a great way to go. They have things called vaults, spaces or wallets, depending on which company you're with. These are little subfolders of your main account. You can name each subfolder with, for example, *Holiday Next Summer*, and lodge the money automatically or manually. I use these vaults for all my annual bills, so for example, I have one called *Home Insurance*, one called *Bins*, one called *Holidays* and so on. Each month when I get paid I put some money into each so when these annual bills or expenses come up I have enough to cover them.

I strongly suggest you automate this – you want to make the decision once, you don't want to make it once a month to transfer money because if you do you can be sure some months it just won't happen.

4. Accepting that you need to multitask

Some goals will be easy to work towards while others will need a little more calculation and maybe even some advice. But it's important that you identify all the goals. A good financial plan is about identifying each goal in isolation and then bringing them all together. Work on each of them individually but think about them collectively.

For example, if you were to say 'I want to retire early and I want to clear the mortgage', then these are two different goals. The easier one to comprehend is that you simply pay a little extra off the mortgage each month and it will be gone sooner. What most people fail to realise is that if you put extra into your pension each month, you could reach retirement sooner and use some of your pension lump sum to clear the balance of the mortgage. This way you get the taxman's help to achieve both of your goals and your money works harder for you. This is a perfect example of knowing the goals but taking a holistic approach.

Sometimes a new client will come to us and say, 'I just want to look at my pension,' or 'I just want to invest some money.' We explain that we will look at everything individually but we must also take the holistic approach as all your goals do interact with each other. In other words, we won't take on a private client if they want us to only look at one thing for them – we take them on in full or not at all.

5. Using different tools for different goals

Knowing *when* you want to achieve a particular goal is one of the most important things in financial planning. If the goal is to be achieved in the short term – considered fewer than five years – then you use short-term vehicles for it. A short-term vehicle is a bank account, credit union or An Post account. I know interest rates are awful but you just have to put up with them.

If the goal is long term, i.e. longer than five years, then you use a long-term vehicle such a no-brainer 60:40 portfolio. These investment vehicles are called no-brainer as they stem from some research done on certified financial analysts (CFA) worldwide. The CFAs were asked what a person without a financial adviser/planner/wealth manager who wanted to invest their money should put it into. The answer was the 60:40 portfolio, where 60 per cent of your money goes into a really well-diversified basket of shares and you buy a little bit of thousands of companies. When we do these for clients it would not be unusual for their investment to have exposure to 5,000 or 6,000 different companies. The other 40 per cent of your money is invested in world corporate and government bonds, which is where you loan your money to governments and companies.

The shares are there to give you the growth; the bonds are there to dilute the risk. Some people ask that if they are getting the growth from shares, then why put the bonds in at all? The reason is for sleep. For most people, the risk of being invested 100 per cent is too scary. Their money would go up and down so much that they would lose sleep and most likely pull the plug at the wrong time for the wrong reason.

We need to turn the volume up on the risk when looking at long-term goals because of inflation. In simple interest terms, if something costs €10,000 today and inflation (that is the cost of basket of goods) runs at 2 per cent per annum that item will cost €11,000 in five years' time. However, if you put your money into a bank account and somehow managed to get 0.5 per cent interest, ignoring tax and again using simple interest, your bank balance will only have grown to €10,250. Your money will have lost €750 of purchasing power. You can put up with this when the goal is fewer than five years but longer than that and your money will take a much bigger hit. So we need to turn up the risk a little by buying shares in order to try and protect the purchasing power of our money. The returns need to be at least greater than inflation over long periods of time.

A typical example of people using a short-term vehicle for a long-term goal is child benefit. People diligently save their children's allowance each month in order to pay for college only to find it falls short by the time they get there.

The figure we use in private practice for college costs is €12,500 per annum – that is the expected cost to the parents if the child lives away from home, so for a four-year degree it will cost €50,000 per child.

Imagine your child was born 18 years ago today and is about to start college. If you had invested €140 per month (I know child benefit has not been as much as this for the past 18 years but let's keep it simple), put this money in a bank account and somehow managed to get 1 per cent per annum interest after taxes on it for the past 18 years it would be worth €33,117 today. So you would be roughly €17,000 short on their college expenses.

If you had stuck it in a 60:40 portfolio and managed to get 4 per cent net of taxes and charges you would have €44,182 today, which means you would be about €6,000 short.

However, if you invested in a very popular fund that was available in Ireland 18 years ago, then you would have €72,338 today. This shows you why it's important to use the right vehicle for the goal.

A typical long-term goal is a pension. The biggest mistake I see people making here is not putting as much as they can into a company pension plan. Typically, the more they pay in the more the employer puts in. So, for example, you put in 3 per cent they put in 3 per cent, and if you put in 5 per cent they put in 5 per cent. There is usually a point at which the employer stops but if this is you and you're not taking the max off your employer then that is as stupid as not accepting a pay rise. Fix it.

There are common misconceptions about pensions. People sometimes ask me whether they should invest in a pension or a 60:40. You can invest your pension in a 60:40 portfolio. Pensions are just savings policies with serious tax breaks attached to them. People who try to save for retirement not using pensions are making life much harder on themselves than it needs to be. A pension basically allows you to save for your retirement using your before-tax income instead of your after-tax income.

Putting €100 per month into a savings policy would use up €200 of income if you're on the higher rate of tax – yes, I'm rounding up here. But you have to earn €200 and pay 50 per cent tax to be left with €100 after tax. Putting the money into your pension means you get to do it *before* the taxman takes their money. If you put €200 directly into your pension and you pay tax at the higher rate, your take-home pay would only go down by €120.

Pensions are often seen as complex but they're as complicated as you want them to be. My recommendation is you keep them simple by remembering they are just a savings plan that gets great tax benefits and you're making life twice as hard on yourself if you try to fund for your retirement without using them.

6. Working out what works for you

Once you've identified extra money from your spending rules to put towards your goals and prioritised your goals, put them all into short-, medium- and long-term brackets. Then it's time to start thinking about the tools at your disposal. How do you set these things up and what tricks are there to keep you safe in the investing world?

The first and most important thing is that when it comes to investing and pensions, time is your friend, and the longer you invest the more chance you have for a positive return.

If you invested a lump sum into a 60:40 portfolio for one year, you would have a 25 per cent chance of losing money. If you invested in it for three years, there is a 15 per cent chance you would lose money. Five years and there is a 0.4 per cent chance you would lose money. In other words a lump sum invested in a 60:40 portfolio has, based on historical data, got a 99.6 per cent chance of a positive return over five years. Leave it longer again and we have yet to experience a seven-or-more-year period where you would have lost money in a standard 60:40 portfolio. When people ask why, if shares are where the return comes from, they don't just go 100 per cent in shares, the reason is because of this seven-year period. There has never been a seven-or-more-year period where you would have lost money in a 60:40. There has, however, been a 21-year period where a 100 per cent share portfolio would have lost you money.

Stock markets go up and down, we know this. We also know that every three to five years on average there is what the media call a stock-market crash, but what I prefer to call a temporary decline. That's because it's a decline and it's temporary and 80 per cent of temporary declines will fully recover within three years.

Time is our friend because it flushes out the bad years but it's also our friend because of compounding – we saw this with Warren Buffet earlier in the book. You need to allow your investments time to breathe but you also need to allow them time to accrue interest on interest, i.e. compounding.

A really important fact is that it's all about time in the market, not timing. You should never try to guess the market. If there's a 25 per cent chance that a 60:40 portfolio is going to lose money in any given year, that means there's a 75 per cent chance it will make money. If you try to time when you put your money in and wait for the so-called 'bottom of the market', you should know that no bell will ring to tell to jump in now and that there is a 75 per cent chance you'll miss out on a positive year.

If your pension or investment is set up right then you should be spread across thousands of companies. This means next year you'll have exposure to the best companies, the worst companies and everything in between but the stats remain that you have a 75 per cent of a positive return. A great example of this was the day Pfizer announced their Covid-19 vaccine. If you had €100 in Pfizer shares, by the end of that day your shares were worth €114. But if you owned €100 in shares in Zoom, by the end of the same day your Zoom shares were worth €95. But if you were invested in the entire market, you had a good day overall. Diversification is your friend.

When it comes to getting your money to work harder for you, keep it simple: put your money in when you have it, take it out when you need it and hope there is a long time in between. If there is then you have a very strong chance of making money. Make sure you spread it out across lots of different shares, set it up right at the start and invest and forget.

7. Taking action

If you're ready to set up an investment or a pension, what do you actually do? Right now in Ireland there are not many online options to do this really well. Some of the big companies have what's called direct sales channels so you can get in touch with them and they will have an adviser go through everything with you. The issue here is that the adviser can only give you advice on that particular company's products so as Henry Ford said, you can have any colour as long as it's black. And don't be fooled into thinking that the in-house adviser will save you money. These big pension and investment houses do large volumes of business through financial advisers and therefore if a client goes direct, they tend not to undercut the adviser who works for themselves. Instead they simply take the money they would have paid the adviser for themselves.

You can walk into your bank and they usually have somebody there who can help you but again, the banks tend only to deal with one provider. Sometimes the bank owns the pension/investment house so you're back to the any-colour-you-want-as-long-as-it's-black situation. You could navigate the paperwork yourself, but most people feel that at least for the form-completion element they need some assistance in choosing the correct product and funds.

Another option is to talk to your HR department or your boss. Every company needs to designate a PRSA provider. This basically means that if they don't have a pension in work and you come looking for one, your company doesn't have to contribute to it but they need to facilitate you paying for one through your wages and give you access to an adviser. People are sometimes shy about approaching their boss about this but believe me you're doing them a favour because if they don't have this set up they can be fined. Your boss or HR department can put you in touch with the designated PRSA provider or, if you have a pension, they will have a relationship with pension-providers.

Another option is to get a financial planner yourself. Talk to your friends, colleagues and family and ask them who they use. We tend as a society not to chat about who our financial planner is, but getting a personal recommendation is by far the best way to go. If all else fails, you can find a list of all the CFPs in Ireland on the FPSB website.

Once you know what you need, setting up a pension is actually very straightforward: you need proof of who you are and where you live and your PPSN [personal public service number] evidence and are then given an application form to complete. If the money is to be put into the pension or investment monthly then the form will have a direct-debit mandate for you to complete and the money is simply collected each month. If it's a lump sum, some people still go old school and give a cheque or bank draft, but most people transfer the money electronically these days.

How do I invest money – what do I ask my adviser/the sales-person/the bank official for?

Whether you decide to deal direct, with a self-employed adviser, through a HR contact or a certified financial planner, the things you want to know are the same across the board.

The most important thing is that you like the person you're dealing with. A great question to ask when you are shopping around for financial help is, *Would I send my elderly mother to them for advice?* If you wouldn't, then run a mile.

When it comes to products you want to know how much you'll be paying in fees. An adviser is required to tell you in monetary terms how much they will be paid in commissions. They will also break down the fees for you.

Typically on any pension, investment or long-term savings plan, there are two types of charges: an annual management fee and an allocation rate. An annual management fee is a percentage of the pot that is taken – it would not be unusual to see annual management fees of 1.5 per cent per annum. So if you have €100,000 invested, they will take a total of 1.5 per cent or €1,500 in charges out of that. An allocation charge or rate is a charge on the money that is going in. So if you get an allocation rate of 95 per cent and you invest €100,000, only 95 per cent of it will actually be invested – in other words, they will take 5 per cent or €5,000 off it when it's going in. Run from anybody who is not giving you 100 per cent allocation; entry costs like this should be a thing of the past but unfortunately they are not. Be really clear when asking about charges and again, if the person you're dealing with is anything less than totally upfront, open and honest – run a mile.

Exit penalties are something else you should be aware of. Sometimes if you take the money out in the first five years you'll be charged a percentage of what you take out. So, for example, they might hit you with a 3 per cent penalty. This is not usually an issue as you should not be going in without the intent of staying for five-plus years anyway but it's worth checking whether it's possible to get out without penalty if you need to.

These things are only as complicated as you allow them to become – remember, done is better than perfect. Get started on improving your long-term financial future by taking one step at a time, but don't lose momentum and don't do what lots of people do, which is to bite off more than they can chew, become disheartened and then dump the entire project. Do it bit by bit.

BRINGING IT ALL TOGETHER

What I have tried to convey in this book is that our relationship with money is an important element of how we manage our money but also that we can change how we manage that relationship for the better. Learning and being open to learning is a key element, as is teaching others, including your kids – remember, we don't truly grasp a concept until we have taught it to somebody! The section around how we teach kids about money should be relevant to you regardless of whether you have kids in your life or not. Seeing how they can learn simplifies money to a level that makes it even easier for us to understand and grasp. Recognising our personality types is another element of our learning, but realising we can be all the different types of personality depending on what stage of our financial journey we are on also reminds us that we can change and adapt if we choose to.

Money is a very personal thing. It provides us with security, fun, education and the basics such as food. How we manage our money will make us either very happy or incredibly stressed. But please remember that we can change our relationship with money every single day. Every time we take out our phones to tap and pay for something or we sign up to a new online subscription, we need to be conscious of what we are doing and repeatedly asking ourselves, *Is this adding value to my life or could I be using this money in a better way?*

You have a choice: you can be good with money or you can choose to ignore it. Being good means you control it, but beware – you might think ignoring it means it doesn't control you, but it does. Make a decision *now* to do little things to get on top of your finances, to make small improvements. Regular, little changes will turn into big results. Don't try to do it all in one go: you'll trip up and feel like you failed and you'll run the risk of not getting back at it again.

And don't be afraid to get things wrong – every shot we miss teaches us something.

Should you get help?

I'm a financial planner. When I have a problem with my teeth I go to a dentist, I don't ask my mate what I should do, I don't google it, I don't pull my tooth myself. So find yourself a good planner is my advice. One you trust, one who is transparent and one you would send your elderly mother to. Don't be afraid of high fees because if they are the right fit they will be worth their weight in gold to your long-term financial future. But even if you do go to a planner, keep educating yourself on money, keep talking to pals and reading the money pages. It puts you in the driving seat and makes for more productive meetings with that planner.

REMEMBER – MONEY ISN'T EVERYTHING

wrote this final bit before I even had this book deal. I thought about how best to fit it in here, but think it's just best to include it as it was written. My dad died on 7 December 2020, and I wrote this at some point during that week.

Dad died. He had been in hospital for months, and we realised in the last few weeks that he wasn't coming out again. We were lucky in that we got to see him several times. I can count about six times since October that we were invited in to say our last goodbyes.

Up until four or five days before he died, he was still engaging and talking away to us. When your dad is in that position you just want to be there, but you also want to help. I'm not a doctor so I was not of any use in that perspective. Yes, I attended meetings with doctors with my mam as a support. But I'm not medically trained, so it was just that: support.

Then Dad asked me to do something, and I realised I could help. He asked me to bring him up to date on his finances. The office helped, and I brought in his documents to his bedside. It came down to one document – all of my dad's financial success, failures, diligence and sacrifices were all on one page in front of us both, and it was then that it hit me just how little importance money has in the last days of our lives.

He didn't care what was on the paper; he just wanted me to do the work so that I could answer one question for him: 'Will Mam be okay financially?'

That was it. The numbers didn't matter. He just wanted reassurance that I had looked through everything and was happy that she would be financially secure. Once I told him that she would be fine and gave him reassurance by breaking down how much extra she could spend each month without ever running out of money, our 'meeting' was over.

Here was my dad, dying, and he just wanted to know whether he had done things well enough financially in his lifetime to leave his wife okay after he was gone. The discussion around his money lasted less than 90 seconds. That was it.

For me, somebody who works with money all day every day, it gave me great joy to be able to put his mind completely at ease; but it also reminded me that, in the end, money is not the important part of life.

I love you, Dad.

FAQ

host an Insta Live every Saturday, during which people can submit financial questions and get an immediate answer. I often receive the same questions week in, week out – and sometimes regular watchers ask if I'm not bored by getting exactly the same query over and over again. But the answer is, I'm not. If people are asking, it's because they don't know the answer; and if I can help, I want to. There's nothing boring to me about that. Below, I've tried to take the most common questions and group them into sections; you can read through them all or jump to the section that interests you (although I hope you don't find any bits of them boring either!). You may even find yourself so interested that you tune into my next Saturday Insta Live (@eoin_mcgee).

General

Q: Why should you only buy a house if you plan on living there for 15+ years?
A: Statistically in 15+ years the value of the house will have risen, meaning you can ignore the short-term ups and downs.

Q: What does CID mean?
A: Contract of indefinite duration, basically a contract with no end date.

Q: Is it a good idea to buy a house share with family?
A: The only way this is going to work is if there is a strong written agreement between everyone about what the outcome looks like when things go wrong and right.

Q: How do banks calculate self-employed income?
A: Most use a three-year average.

Q: Why don't you recommend strict budgets for controlling spending?

A: Life is too short to be living restrictively. Life also isn't linear, so a strict budget makes you feel like you fail every time life happens.

Q: What is the best way to take money out of a limited company as a sole director?

A: Pension, then look at entrepreneurial and retirement relief too.

Q: If you plan to upsize a house within five years, is it worth overpaying the mortgage rather than saving in a bank?

A: Keep your options (cash) in your hands.

Q: Do banks consider salary scales and potential earnings?

A: Some banks take pay scales of public-sector workers into account.

Q: Advice on pensions for stay-at-home parents?

A: If you're not paying tax then just save.

Q: When does it make financial sense to retire early?

A: When the time you can afford to comes together with the moment that you want to.

Q: What is the most efficient way to build wealth in Ireland?

A: Spend less than you earn.

Q: Is an allocation fee only paid upon entering the investment or every year?

A: Allocation rate is a charge every time you put money in.

Q: College savings for kids went down in value, is this normal?

A: Depends what you invested in.

Q: How do mortgage brokers earn money? Is it upfront of after you buy a house?

A: Some charge fees and get a commission when you draw down the mortgage. Some just work on commission. Don't be afraid of either, just look for complete transparency.

Q: Do you think we will see something like austerity again?

A: I think that would be destructive to the future recovery of the economy.

Q: What qualifications/title should I look for when looking for a financial adviser?

A: Ideally get a CFP [certified financial planner]. But most important is using somebody you trust.

Q: Starting my first 'adult' job, any tips?

A: This is the biggest pay rise you're likely to get in your entire career. You're most likely going from hourly wages to a salary. Remember, you survived on your wages before. Decide now to save and not to get accustomed to using your full salary every month. Don't let lifestyle creep kick in.

Q: The best way to get a credit score?

A: Credit scores are an American thing; they have not taken off here. The IT/ structure is there for them but they are not widely used. Just save consistently each month.

Q: Any tips on finding a financial adviser?

A: Ask your family and friends who they use.

Q: I get a car allowance from work. Does BIK [benefit in kind] come into play?

A: There is no BIK on a company car if it's all electric and cost less than €50k.

Q: How much do I need to allow for solicitors + extra costs when deciding a budget for buying a house?

A: General rule of thumb is use 5 per cent of the purchase price. So €15k on a house worth €300k.

Q: Tips for organising money?

A: Loads of apps out there for this. Test some of them out and see which one suits you.

Q: At 25 years old, should I save for a mortgage or start pension contributions?

A: Why not both?

Q: Keeping finances separate or combining them when married?

A: Different strokes for different folks. Communication is key here and deciding what works best for you both.

Q: What are your thoughts on mortgage competition in Ireland?

A: Competition is great in every market. We are small and not very attractive to new lenders.

Mortgage

Q: Can I get a mortgage if I am an independent contractor?

A: Yes, if you have a minimum of two years of accounts. Get a broker.

Q: Are Rebuilding Ireland and Help to Buy for first-time buyers only?

A: Yes, but the shared equity scheme coming down the line may include certain second-time buyers.

Q: How much of a deposit would you recommend having before talking to a bank about a mortgage?

A: Minimum 10 per cent.

Q: Pay a lump sum off a mortgage to reduce term or up monthly payments?

A: Most probably neither, though it depends on each situation. Very rarely is it a good idea to do either of these, due to the opportunities lost – that is, there will likely always be something else you could have done with that money that would have better benefitted your long-term financial future.

Q: Does the value of land count towards the deposit for a mortgage?

A: In most cases, yes. Provided your belief of what it's worth is the same belief as the market has of what it's worth.

Q: Betting activity on my bank account, do I need to wait for a mortgage?

A: Having betting activity on your account isn't an automatic 'no'. It's just an easy excuse if they don't want to give you the money. Talk to a good broker first.

Q: Can I get a mortgage for a holiday home abroad if I'm working in Ireland?

A: Not from an Irish bank (any more) but a foreign bank may entertain you.

Q: I have a mortgage at 2.9 per cent fixed, is it worth changing?

A: Depends how much is left on the mortgage: for every €100,000 over 20 years a 1 per cent reduction will save about €50 per month. Be careful of breakage fees.

Q: Can you get mortgage approval without the 10 per cent deposit?

A: Possibly, if the bank sees that you'll make it there by the time you want to draw down the mortgage. But beware: you need to pay for solicitors, valuations and furnishing the place, and 10 per cent won't cut it, I'm afraid.

Q: Can you get a mortgage in Ireland if you live and work abroad?

A: Yes, but you'll need a very large deposit.

Q: If I buy a new car on HP [hire purchase] will it affect any future mortgage application?

A: It can have a big impact or zero impact, it depends on the maths.

Q: Does it look bad in the bank's eyes if most of the money in your FTB deposit is from gifted funds?

A: Not really, but you'll need to prove 'ability to repay'. This is only shown by you regularly saving, paying rent or a combo of both.

Q: Does a car loan need to be cleared to get a mortgage?

A: Not always but it can significantly reduce how much you can borrow.

Q: Selling my current house, should I re-mortgage or apply as a second-time buyer for a new house?

A: When you sell your house you're required to clear the mortgage on it. There is no way around it.

Q: For a mortgage of €350k how much should I save each month?

A: A €350k mortgage will cost under €1.5k per month (for 30 years) so I'd suggest you would need to be saving at least €2k per month to price ability to repay.

Q: Where to start to get a mortgage?

A: Start by saving and clearing up your bank statements.

Q: How much do you recommend spending on monthly mortgage repayments as percentage of salary?

A: You shouldn't spend more than 35 per cent.

Q: When a bank is looking at the ability to repay a mortgage, do they look at savings potential (rent)?

A: The bank will take the total of savings and rent into account when looking at your ability to repay.

Q: Ireland has higher mortgage rates compared to EU, why?

A: Banks here suggest this is due to several factors, which include:

1. Regulations: mortgage providers have to hold cash against money they give out. Banks here are required to hold more than some countries in Europe.
2. We have one of the highest default rates in Europe.
3. It takes longer than average to repossess a house here.

Q: Any downside to overpaying mortgage when on a variable rate?
A: It's the lost opportunity I'd be worried about, i.e. what else could you be doing with the extra money that would make more financial sense.

Q: If I qualify for the full HTB [help to buy], do I still need to show this amount in my savings?
A: Not necessarily but you need to prove you're able to pay back the mortgage each month and this is easiest proved by showing them your savings record, but proof of rent paid helps too.

Q: Are smaller fortnightly mortgage repayments better than full monthly repayments in the long run?
A: There are 13 four-week periods in the year, so you make an extra month's repayment every year.

Q: Joint income of around €200k, both early 40s, currently renting. What is a sensible mortgage?
A: I'd conservatively guess that you have a take-home income of €8k p/m. I wouldn't commit more than 35 per cent of this to commitments such as loans. That means in total on all loans you could afford to spend €2.85k p/m. If you have no other loan commitments, this would serve a mortgage of around €600k over 25 years. This is an absolute limit, not a target.

Q: Are mortgage LTV [loan to value] exemptions from banks usually all given out in the first quarter of the year?
A: Nope. But they are like the lotto in terms of when to time your application.

Q: Planning on selling in a few years. Should you take the shortest mortgage term you can afford?
A: Be careful about building a plan revolving around the 'need' to sell in a few years' time. A lot (such as property prices) is outside your control with such a plan. You would have more options with more savings and a smaller mortgage when moving.

Q: FTB [first-time buyer], where to start?

A: Go to a good broker, that's like walking into all the banks at once.

Q: Should I sell one or both of my rentals to pay off my house faster? Both in positive equity.

A: A good financial planner's job is to build a financial plan that gives you absolute clarity on the long-term impact of financial decisions (like this) that you're making today.

Q: What do banks look into for a mortgage?

A: They ask for six months of statements and if they see anything dodgy they go back further. Sometimes going back is to prove a positive rather than a negative.

Q: How much should we be saving monthly for a €500k mortgage as a FTB?

A: A €500k mortgage over 30 years will cost you €2,108 p/m. You should show the bank that between rent and savings you can afford a total of €2,750 p/m.

Q: Any tips for getting a decent mortgage as a sole applicant?

A: Look for a good broker and have a look at Rebuilding Ireland home loans.

Q: Borrowing €220k, purchase price of house €290k, will I get the HTB scheme?

A: It needs to be a new house or a self-build and you need to be borrowing more than 70 per cent. You also need to have paid enough tax in the last four years (it's a refund of taxes paid).

Q: Mortgage for a 51-year-old on his own. Where to start? Is it possible?

A: Tougher because the loan has to be paid back over a shorter timeframe, which pushes up the monthly payments.

Q: FTB: should we go to a broker or do it ourselves?

A: Broker all the way.

Q: FTB benefits of using a broker rather than doing it yourself?

A: Why look at the menu in one restaurant before you eat when you can get somebody else (a broker) to see what you want and look at all the restaurants to get you the perfect meal?

Q: Second-time buyer, hoping for an exemption for a deposit next year. What are the chances?

A: Depends on two things: the first is in your control and it's all about how well you present your finances to the bank; the second is out of your control and depends on how the bank is doing at the time.

Q: How do you work out the total interest on a mortgage?

A: 1. Take the number of years on the mortgage and multiply it by 12; 2. Take the repayment and multiply it by the answer you got; 3. Take the answer in 2 and deduct the mortgage you took out.

e.g. 1. 30-year mortgage by 12 = 360 payments; 2. Payment on a 3 per cent mortgage of €100k is €421.60 p/m (421.6 × 360 = €151,776); 3. €151,776 − €100,000 mortgage = €51,776 in interest.

Q: Can AIP amount be increased if you get a pay rise?

A: Totally.

Q: Would cash lodgements into savings account negatively affect a mortgage application?

A: It wouldn't be a negative. Just be sure to explain it upfront and don't have them coming to you to ask about it.

Savings

Q: I have savings sitting in the credit union to build my house, should I move it?

A: If you're going to build in the next five years leave it where it is. If not, then get it invested in a long-term vehicle.

Q: What should I do with my savings?

A: Apply the five-year rule. If you're going to spend it in the next five years, then put it in a bank/credit union account. If you're not, then invest it (60:40 portfolio).

Q: Should I have a joint account with my husband? All of our savings are in my personal account.

A: Sounds like you've control of the run-away money/f**k-off fund – why would you want to change that?

Q: State savings to save long term for children's college education, yay or nay?

A: Saving for kids' education is a long-term goal. State savings are a short-term vehicle. You don't use a short-term vehicle for a long-term goal.

Q: Very bad at saving money, any advice on how to be a better saver?

A: You're in the habit of saving or you're not. It's a choice you make. Decide today to start saving, anything, it doesn't matter how small. Just start!

Q: Just paid off the mortgage, any tips on best to save the rest of our money?

A: Don't allow yourself to adjust your life (that you start using what was the mortgage money on 'stuff'). Get stuck into saving it straight away; maybe get advice on putting it into a pension.

Q: Are prize bonds worth buying?

A: How long will the money be 'resting in the account, Dougal?' If it's less than five years then they are harmless enough. But only because bank deposit rates are crap anyway.

Inheritance

Q: Inheriting money, would it be better to lump that into a pension or drip-feed it in?

A: A well-constructed, well-diversified investment/pension will go up in three to four years. Obviously, we don't know which the 'bad' year is going to be and they may even run one after the other, there is no way of knowing. If you drip-feed money into an investment/pension and things go down as you're putting it in then it was a good idea. Based on the odds above, there is a 75 per cent chance a lump is the right thing to do in any given year. I prefer straight in, but I do use drip-feeding when a client is very nervous.

Q: If you receive more than €335k from a parent, do you pay tax on the remainder or total?

A: You pay pax on the remainder as the first €335k is tax free.

Q: I was left shares by a late family member, am I liable for tax?

A: Depends who the family member was to you; if it's your parents and they are worth more than €335k then yes, you are. If it's an uncle or aunt, then anything above €32.5k will be taxable and anybody else will be taxed above €16,250. If you have got a gift/inheritance in the past from any of these groups, this needs to be taken into account when working out the tax.

Q: Can parents gift you money to use towards a house deposit? Is there a maximum amount?

A: You can get a total of €335k in your lifetime from your parents. They can also give you 3k a year (€3k from Mammy and €3k from Daddy).

Q: If a parent leaves you the family home in a will, do you have to pay taxes?

A: Provided the value of everything you inherit is less than €335k then no. Sometimes there is a 'family home' exemption but not typically for adult children.

Q: I received a lump sum from my uncle 10 years ago, never declared it.

A: Depends on how much it was. You can get €32.5k from your uncle before tax kicks in. But it should be declared.

Q: With gift tax (€335k to kids) is it per child? Can you give them non-liquid gifts e.g. a house?

A: It's €335k per child and is the total from both parents that they can get. It can be cash or property. It's all assets. Sometimes the family home is exempt if certain criteria is met.

Q: Can I still get €3k cash from each parent if they have a joint account?

A: You can get €3k from each parent. It doesn't matter from which account you receive the funds as long as it's evident who you're receiving the money from.

Tax

Q: If you're given land by a family member, is that family member liable for tax?

A: Potentially they are liable.

Q: Do you pay tax on Airbnb income?

A: If you make money, then you pay tax.

Q: If I rent my house out do I pay tax on any profit after the mortgage is paid?

A: You pay tax on any rent after allowable expenses. The full mortgage payment is not allowable, only the interest part of the mortgage. This catches loads of people out.

Q: Buying a house for €100k under selling price from a family member, are there any tax implications?

A: The reduction is a 'gift' for tax purposes.

Q: Do you have to pay tax on stocks bought through an online banking app?

A: If you make money, you pay tax.

Q: If I win the lottery will I pay tax?

A: Lottery pay-outs here are tax free to the winner.

Q: Will I pay tax on the sale of my private home and/or my investment property?

A: The sale of your home is not subject to tax. If you didn't make money on the investment property there won't be tax either.

Q: What's the difference between capital gains tax and exit tax?

A: About 8 per cent.

Q: Can you explain how CGT [capital gains tax] is calculated? Looking to sell a property.

A: You pay 33 per cent on the difference between the price the house was when you bought it versus the price you sell it for. You can add big expenses to the original price if you can prove those costs.

Q: Does getting married affect your tax? And how?

A: If your partner isn't using all of their 20 per cent threshold they can give you some (not all) of it. If you die there is no inheritance tax between spouses. Finally there are other advantages, such as the 'love' thing.

Q: Can a child gift a parent a cash amount without tax implications?

A: Any person in the state can give another person in the state €3k per year without tax implications.

Q: How to avoid paying tax on ETF [exchange traded funds] gains? Invested in ETFs which I plan to hold onto for retirement.

A: Why didn't you put them with your pension? No tax in there and tax relief on the way in.

Q: Can you get tax back from income protection schemes?

A: Yes.

Q: Tax Relief on WFH [working from home]. If your name is not on the bills, is this an issue?

A: It's a problem. The bill needs to be in your name.

Q: If you and your spouse are both working from home and both names are on the bills can you both claim tax relief?

A: Nice try but no. But there is no reason why your accountant couldn't argue you claim more of the bill. Both employers could give you €3.20 per day.

Q: Partner on €24k, I'm on €40k. Will my tax bill go down if we get married and are jointly assessed?

A: Most likely as in your case they should still have some unused tax credits they can give you.

Pension

Q: I am going to be made redundant in a year, what pension questions should I be asking?

A: You put money into your pension for the previous tax year if a certain date has not passed (31st October following tax year). Given you'll be getting a lump sum from redundancy, if you have the cash now, I would ask your HR/payroll to calculate what your max contribution is for last year and I would suggest that you pay that now. Do the same for the following years until you leave the company.

Q: Is it worth setting up a private pension if on agency work?

A: Yes, and bring it with you to your next job.

Q: If you pay into your pension, do you play less tax?

A: If you're on the higher rate of tax (40 per cent) and you pay €100 into your pension you'll pay €40 less tax, which means your take-home pay will only go down by €60. If you pay 20 per cent tax, then it costs €80 to put €100 into your pension.

Q: Does my employer have to give me a pension?
A: Your employer is required to provide access to a PRSA and to facilitate deduction from your salary to pay into it but they are not required to pay into it themselves.

Q: When should I start my pension?
A: You're never too young or old to start a pension.

Q: What is the difference between putting extra money into an investment fund vs into a pension?
A: Put your money into a pension, then your pension into an investment fund.

Q: Are the pensions benefits better as a sole trader or ltd?
A: There may be a bit of paperwork involved in becoming a limited company, but the pension entitlements are much better.

Q: Can you set up a personal pension in Ireland while working abroad?
A: You can but you shouldn't bother. Pensions are about tax relief and tax-free growth. If you're not paying tax here, you won't get any tax advantages.

Q: Employer pension contribution, does this apply to your personal allowance?
A: Only if it's a PRSA [personal retirement savings account].

Q: My employer is paying into my pension, if I leave that job does the pension come with me?
A: It's called 'vested' rights – some employers have it set up that if you leave in the first two years you don't get their contribution. Other employers let you have their money if you leave within the first two years.

Q: AVCs [additional voluntary contributions] – I have been doing them for the last five years, should I continue?
A: They are a great idea; you still use the 60:40 portfolio if you aren't getting advice and you get the same tax benefits of any pension.

Q: Self-administered pension, is it worth it?

A: Depends on what you want to do with it. Lots of people have the best intentions and then end up sitting on cash.

Q: What is the max tax-free lump sum you can get from your pension?

A: You get a lump sum from your pension of either 25 per cent of your pot or up to 1.5 times your final salary. The first €200k of any lump sum is tax free and the next €300k is taxed at 20 per cent.

Q: What is the earliest age you can draw on your pension?

A: Some are at age 50 and others at age 60.

Q: Can we do something with a dormant pension?

A: Make sure it's still invested. It should still be 'doing something'.

Q: Separate pensions, should they be added together? Or what is the best option?

A: I don't advise mixing old work pensions with new work pensions mainly because keeping them separate means you can access them at different times in the future.

Q: Is it better to invest in stocks and shares than a pension?

A: Invest your pension in stocks and shares, you won't pay tax on the profit then.

Q: At age 57 is it more beneficial to put extra money into my pension for five years or save it?

A: When it comes to pensions the questions should always be: 'Is there any reason I shouldn't put this money into my pension?' There is no other way around it.

Q: I have a public sector PRSA [personal retirement savings account] – is this different to AVCs in any way?

A: Rules are the same.

Q: Working abroad with no pension started, how do I start one.

A: You need to start it in the country you're paying tax in. Get advice locally.

Q: Is a pension at 40 a good idea?

A: The fact that you're 40 makes no odds, when is getting free money from the government and a pay rise from your boss a bad idea?

Q: Max out pension cap in salary before opening separate savings accounts?

A: Depends what stage in life you're at and what your short-/medium-term goals are. General rule of thumb is: if you know you won't need the money until you retire then reduce your tax bill today and stick it in the pension.

Q: Just moved jobs. €80k in old pension. Take out a PRB [personal retirement bond] or move it to the new company?

A: Or leave it in the old pension. I would usually go with leaving it where it is or moving it to a PRB. Moving it to your new job's pension isn't something that I would recommend as it complicates things down the line.

Q: Been offered a 2 per cent salary increase or 3 per cent pension increase, Help!

A: Let's imagine you're on €100k and 40 years old. If you take the pay rise it's worth €2k a year before tax. So that's €1k per year after tax and if you save that €1k for 25 years at 4 per cent you'll accumulate €42k. Take the pension increase of €3k.

Q: I'm a low-grade worker in the public sector, should I get an AVC pension?

A: If you can afford it, yes. It's a great way of saving money even if you only get €2 tax back for every €10 you put in.

Q: If I want to contribute more than match for my pension, should I do it through a work scheme or elsewhere?

A: Big group schemes often get cheaper AVC plans than you'll get privately.

But check because it's not always the case. Some people prefer to do it privately for many reasons, one being that your work won't know what you're doing.

Q: What per cent pension should I do? 36 years old and currently do 7 per cent to get a match.

A: At your age bracket you're allowed to do 20 per cent so get as close to that as you can.

Q: Career break the last three years, should I still be paying into my pension?

A: If you're not paying tax then no.

Q: Want to start a pension at 40, who is best to go with/ start with?

A: Find yourself a good, independent CFP.

Loans and overdrafts

Q: I owe money on a student loan, should I replay loan solely or split between loan payment and savings?

A: Depends on the rate on the loan, but without getting too bogged down I'd suggest kill the debt first.

Q: If I have enough money to pay off a car loan in one go, should I do it or continue to pay it monthly?

A: Don't leave yourself short of savings in case 'life' happens next month and you end up having to borrow to cover 'life'. In general, loans are bad.

Q: Should I pay all of all my loan with my savings? They will clear roughly half the loan.

A: You have to be careful about clearing savings completely. I'd also feel a bit robbed if I wasn't getting to clear a loan in full.

Q: Would it be financially wise to buy a car using PCP [personal contract purchase]?

A: I'm not a fan of getting loans for anything. Sometimes we need loans for things, sometimes we want things. But we should never need a loan for something we only want.

Q: My salary has been reduced and the last week of the month I am always in overdraft, is that really bad?

A: Overdrafts are for emergencies. If you're constantly in overdraft then you're constantly in an emergency. Treat it like any other loan and reduce how deep you go into each month until you reach a point where you don't go into it.

Q: Each month I put money into my savings only to go into my overdraft, is this very bad?

A: It's not great. Effectively you're not saving; your overdraft is doing the saving and the banks are charging you for the privilege.

Q: In terms of savings, is it worth moving money from a credit union to a bank with better interest?

A: When it comes to interest get as much as you can, pay as little as you can.

Q: What should your rainy-day fund be?

A: Between three and six months of household income. Three if you've a steady job, six if you don't.

Q: Buy an old car with cash vs a new car on finance?

A: I'm a financial planner, what do you think my answer is going to be? Seriously though, if cars aren't your thing and the old car is reliable, why not?

Q: Occasionally dip into my overdraft, will this affect my mortgage application? Should I get rid?

A: Yes you should 'get rid'. It's crappy debt. It's expensive and you become reliant on it. Overdrafts are for emergencies; if you're constantly in overdraft then the bank will think you're in a constant state of emergency.

Credit cards

Q: €4,000 on a credit card, should I get a loan to clear or pay off what I can as I go?

A: Firstly, do you really hate debt? If you hate it and you're tackling it aggressively move it to an interest-free credit card. Never use the new one and clear it down before the new credit card's interest kicks in.

Investments

Q: If investments are more likely to go up over the years, why not take high-risk investment only?

A: Most people can't handle the ups and downs of higher risk and end up pulling the plug at the wrong time.

Q: Do you pay DIRT or other tax on a 60:40 investment?

A: Generally you pay exit tax at 41 per cent of the profit. If you're paying tax then you're making money.

Q: Is five years long enough to get a decent return from a 60:40 investment?

A: Based on history there is a 99.6 per cent chance of a positive return over five years in a 60:40 portfolio.

Q: Do you pay exit tax on gains made from a pension investment fund?

A: You don't pay tax on the growth in a pension.

Q: Best five- to six-year investment?

A: Invest in (1) you, (2) your family and (3) your future.

Q: Passive or actively managed funds?

A: Passive with a twist is my way.

Q: Is it possible to lose all the money you invest?

A: If it's invested properly, well diversified and excluding any type of fraud, then it will go up and down and sometimes as much as 50 per cent either way with some risky funds. But to lose it all would mean all the companies you own a little bit of would have to go to the wall at the exact same time.

Q: Thoughts on a NTMA [National Treasury Management Agency] 10-year bond?

A: They give the returns of a short-term vehicle like a bank account or credit union account and are not suitable for long-term goals. Use long-term vehicles (like a 60:40 portfolio) for long-term goals and short-term vehicles (bank accounts) for short-term goals of fewer than five years.

Q: What is a 60:40 portfolio?

A: 60 per cent global shares, 40 per cent global bonds, no fuss.

Q: Easiest way to invest S&P 500 fund (outside pension)?

A: Much easier in the US but why only invest in the US stock market? It represents 54 per cent of the financial world but what about the other 46 per cent?

Q: What is the best way to save for a child's future?

A: That is a long-term goal, use a long-term vehicle like the no-brainer 60:40 portfolio.

Q: Can myself and my husband sell our investment property to my pension fund using a pension mortgage?

A: Nope, you have to adhere to the 'arm's length rule', which means you can't buy something with your pension from somebody you're connected to through blood or marriage.

Q: Do you need a lump sum for a 60:40? Or can you start small and put money in weekly?

A: You can invest monthly.

Q: Is 60:40 still a good option? There are a lot of 'it's dead' articles online.

A: I'd be checking out who is writing said articles. I bet they sell their ability to beat the 60:40 portfolio for a living. Remember a 60:40 is for people who don't get advice. If you're paying someone for advice then take it.

Q: Want to invest but I'm risk averse. Any recommendations?

A: I'd suggest that you're not risk averse, you just haven't found the right person who can explain to you how investing properly works. Investing properly is simple, boring and not one bit sexy. We all fear things we don't understand. Get a good financial planner who will help you understand.

Q: Starting a pension and blown away by the different investment options. Any advice?

A: If you don't have an adviser look for the no-brainer 60:40 portfolio (60 per cent global shares, 40 per cent global bonds).

Q: I want to start investing my savings but don't know where to start with the self-assessment tax.

A: If you invest with a life insurance company they look after all the taxes for you (if you invest with a stockbroker or through your banking app, it often means you need to look after taxes yourself).

Life assurance

Q: Life assurance policies when buying a house?

A: Get the cheapest of the cheapest to satisfy the bank and then invest time and money into getting the right one for you and your family. Don't put the family one off until you 'get settled' into the house.

Q: Should you go for life assurance if you already have it with work?

A: Yes, if you need it. If you died yesterday, how much salary are you no longer going to earn that your family are going to have to go without?

Q: Is it good to shop around for life assurance?

A: Absolutely, or better still get a broker.

Income protection

Q: Does income protection cover redundancy?

A: It doesn't cover redundancy; it pays out if your doctor and the product provider's doctors say you're unfit for work due to illness or injury.

Shares

Q: Should I sell my work shares when they mature each year or hold onto them?

A: I've a strong belief that you shouldn't tie your income and wealth to your employer. This is not to get better returns elsewhere it's to dilute the risk you're taking with your life!

GLOSSARY

60/40 portfolio: An investment or pension split between 60 per cent shares and 40 per cent bonds.

Allocation rate: How much of your money in your pension, investment or savings plan gets invested. An allocation rate of 95 per cent means that 5 per cent of the amount you invest is taken as a charge at the start of your investment.

Annual management fee: A periodic charge paid from an investment, savings plan or pension to the fund's investment advisor. The charge is a percentage taken from the full pot.

Annual percentage rate (APR): The interest rate charged on a mortgage or a loan for a whole year. It is a great way of comparing loans against each other.

Approval in principle (AIP): Document stating that the lender has looked at your case for a mortgage and is happy to offer you one, provided that everything you have told them is true and can be backed up with paperwork. A word of warning: the easier it is to get an AIP, the less value I would tend to put on it.

Asset allocation: When you invest long-term, you put money in things like shares and bonds. These are assets. Asset allocation is the term used for how you split your money across the assets.

Austerity: A government's decision to increase taxes, cut spending or do both. These strict policies are usually introduced during a time of economic crisis for a country, in an attempt to control growing public debt.

Auto-enrolment: When individuals who join a company are automatically enrolled in the pension offered without needing to fill out any paperwork to join the scheme. Those who do not want to join would instead have to fill out forms to stop this from happening.

Benefit in kind (BIK): When your boss gives you something that is viewed as a 'reward' for working for them but does not take the form of salary or wages – a company car, for example. The government then taxes you based on the financial value of that 'something'.

Bonds: When you invest long-term, one of the asset classes you can use is bonds. Bonds are effectively you giving a loan of your money to companies or governments. In return, they pay you a coupon each year and, if all goes to plan, they will pay you back your money in one payment at the end of the bond term.

Capital Acquisitions Tax (CAT): The tax you pay when you receive a gift or inheritance over a certain threshold. The rate is currently 33 per cent.

Central Bank: The regulator for the financial services industry in Ireland. It keeps an eye on what is happening in banks and other financial services firms. It also creates rules for the banks to adhere to when it comes to give out mortgages.

Central Credit Register (CRC): Where all the information about any loan over €500 is held. It is run by the Central Bank. You can get a free report from the Central Credit Register, which details what information the banks have about your credit history.

Commodities: An economic good or service that can be invested in. Commodities are typically natural resources, such as oil, gold or coal.

Compound interest: Interest on interest. The addition of interest to the principal sum of a loan, deposit or investment.

Consumer price index: A measure of inflation. It tracks the price of a basket of goods and checks how much it changes on a year-to-year basis.

Cryptocurrency: This is literally the million-dollar question… Potentially it is a digital currency, but it doesn't have all the attributes of a traditional currency, so some people still question its validity as such. Others suggest it is a commodity, while still others suggest it is an asset class of its own. People trying to predict whether usage of crypto will consolidate or completely drop off is a main driver of the fluctuation in price – and crypto users worldwide agreeing once and for all what is actually is will also be a key factor in its longevity or demise.

Deposit Interest Retention Tax (DIRT): The tax you pay on the interest you get for leaving money in a bank account.

Depreciation: Some assets, such as property, tend to go up in value over long periods of time; but others – such as cars – lose value. The money you lose on assets that become less valuable is called depreciation.

Diversification: Spreading your risk while investing. It means splitting the shares that you own across thousands of companies in lots of sectors, industries and countries – to reduce the risk that they could all lose money at the same time. In simple terms, it's the opposite of having all your eggs in one basket; diversification is having lots of eggs in lots of different baskets.

Dow Jones Industrial Average (DJIA): One of the big US stock market indices. It is a collection of the 30 largest US companies based on their financial size.

European Central Bank (ECB): Like our Central Bank but over all of Europe. The ECB sets our monetary policies and interest rates, which influences how much we can borrow.

Eurostoxx 50: This index tracks the largest 50 companies in Europe.

Exceptions: The Central Bank applies mortgage measures that banks must adhere to when lending. The banks can, however, break the rules from time to time, in what is called an exception.

Fintech banks: The word 'fintech' means financial technology, and the two have come together to offer a new type of banking that is typically all online – it's functional, transparent and usually mobile-friendly. High street banks have noticed and are attempting to offer similar services, but they have some catching up to do!

FTSE: An index tracking companies in the UK. The FTSE 100 tracks the largest 100 companies, while the FTSE 250 tracks the largest 250.

Income tax: The tax taken by the government from your wages.

Inflation: The increase or decrease in the value of goods and services. This can go up or down, but the target rate of inflation for Europe is 2 per cent per year.

Interest: The money you receive from a financial institution if you leave your savings with them, or the money you pay when you borrow money.

Investments: Money put away for the medium to long-term. Investments can relate to anything from buying a house to buying a fund that invests in stocks and shares. The objective of an investment is to grow your money.

ISEQ: This index tracks the largest companies in Ireland.

Life cover: This is an insurance policy that pays out in the event of the insured person dying. The amount paid out is based on the amount of cover you choose to take out.

Lifestyle creep: When people get a pay rise, their life usually becomes more expensive. They allow their lifestyle to expand to fill the income they now have, i.e. they allow it to creep upwards to meet their new salary.

Loan-to-income limits: The Central Bank has mortgage measures around how much banks can lend to people when they are approving mortgages. One of the rules, for example, says that somebody cannot borrow more than 3.5 times their income.

Loan-to-value limits: A rule that states that first-time buyers cannot borrow more than 90 per cent of the value of a house, and that second-time buyers cannot borrow more than 80 per cent. These rules can be broken with an exception.

Long-term savings account/plan: When you put money aside on a regular basis and it accumulates over time. When you are investing long-term, it should be in something other than a bank account and should be invested in shares and bonds.

Market capitalisation: If you take the share price of a company and multiply it by the number of shares that exist for that company, you can calculate its market capitalisation.

Moratorium: Where your lender can give you a break from repayments for a period of time, usually three to six months. This is often done if you are sick or have just had a baby.

Negative interest rate: Banks make their profit from the difference between the amount they pay their customers in interest for lodging their money, and the amount they charge the customers who have taken out loans. Because interest rates have been low for a long time now, banks across the world are struggling to make a decent profit on this difference. In very simplistic terms, this explains why some banks have started charging negative interest rates – that is, they will charge you for leaving your savings with them.

Net worth: The value of everything you own, financial and nonfinancial, less the value of all your loans.

Overdraft: Pre-approved credit where you can go into minus numbers on your bank account. Once it is approved you don't need to apply each time. You get charged high interest when you stay in it for long periods of time and should only be used in emergencies.

Pandemic Unemployment Payment (PUP): A social welfare payment that was introduced by government during the COVID-19 health emergency. It is intended to help people who lost their employment during this time, perhaps due to the place where they worked being closed during a lockdown phase in the interest of public health. PUP is paid directly to the recipient by the government, in the same way that other social welfare payments are made.

Pay As You Earn (PAYE): A method of paying your income tax. It is the money that is taken out of your wages and paid every time you are paid.

Pay-related social insurance (PRSI): This is taken from your wages and is effectively an insurance policy. It pays for things like sick pay from the government, if you are out sick.

Pension: A tax-efficient savings plan that helps people save for their retirement.

Personal contract plans (PCPs): A form of hire purchase when financing cars. You don't actually own the car when you get on a PCP. You have the option to rent again at the end of the term or to pay a lump sum and buy the car.

Savings account: A short-term vehicle (less than five years), which can be in the form of a deposit account or a post-office or Credit Union account.

Section 72 plan: A life-insurance policy where the people you leave your money to receive it tax paid, instead of having to pay the inheritance tax on it.

Shares: Pieces of a company. Companies need to raise money at certain times during their growth. They do this by selling parts of the company to the general public of investors.

Simple interest: A straightforward way of calculating interest. It is useful for quick calculations but rarely used in real life. It can relate to loans or growth on investments.

Small gift tax allowance: An amount of money (currently €3,000) that any person in the state can give to any other person in the state in a calendar year. They will not have to pay tax on it and it will not eat into their group inheritance/gift threshold.

Special Saving Incentive Accounts (SSIA): A government incentive launched in 2001–02 to encourage people to save for 5 years. For every €4 you put into your savings, the government would put in €1 as well. When your money went into the account, the government's was added at the same time so that you could see it, and this transparency proved very popular.

Specified illness cover: An insurance policy that pays out a lump sum if you are diagnosed with a listed specified illness. Typical payouts are for things like cancer, heart attack or stroke. The amount paid out is based on the amount of cover you paid for when taking out the plan.

Standard & Poor 500 (S&P 500): An investment index that tracks the 500 largest companies in the US.

Tax relief: When the government offers an incentive in order to encourage the public do things – such as to put money into a pension. The government will give you relief from the requirement to pay tax because you are doing something that they want you to do.

Tracker rate: A repayment rate (usually on a mortgage, but occasionally with other loans) that goes up and down in accordance with the ECB interest rate – in other words, it tracks the ECB rate.

Universal social charge (USC): A tax that is taken from your wages. It replaced both the income levy and the health levy.

Volatility: This is a measure of how rough a ride an investment has taken in the past. It can be useful in guessing how much an investment might go up or down in the future.

Wage subsidy: This was a payment made to businesses who suffered a downturn in income due to the pandemic. Unlike PUP, it was available to businesses that remained open but were not trading at previous levels. The subsidy was to be used to pay the salaries of the staff; employers could choose to top up employees' pay to 100 per cent of their pre-pandemic wage, or just pass on the money they received from the government.